Honda 65, 70 & 90 Owners Workshop Manual

by Jeff Clew

Models covered:

63 cc	Honda 865 (ohc) motorcycle
72 cc	Honda C70 (ohc) scooter
86.7 cc	Honda C200 (ohv) motorcycle
	Honda CM90 (ohv) scooter
89.6 cc	Honda C90 (ohc) scooter
	Honda S90 (ohc) motorcycle
	Honda CM90 (ohc) scooter

First introduced in 1964

ISBN 0 85696 116 7

© J H Haynes and Company Limited 1973

All rights reserved. No part of this book may be reproduced or transmitted in any form or by an means, electronic or mechanical, including photocopying, recording or by any information storage or retrieval system, without permission in writing from the copyright holder.

Printed in England (116 - 8AI)

Haynes

J H HAYNES AND COMPANY LIMITED
SPARKFORD YEOVIL SOMERSET ENGLAND

distributed in the USA by
HAYNES PUBLICATIONS INC.
9421 WINNETKA AVENUE
CHATSWORTH LOS ANGELES
CALIFORNIA 91311 USA

Acknowledgements

Grateful thanks are due to Honda (UK) Limited for the technical assistance given so freely whilst this manual was being prepared. Brian Horsfall gave the necessary assistance with the overhaul and devised many ingenious methods for overcoming the lack of service tools, which are rarely available to the average owner/rider. Les Brazier arranged and took the photographs that accompany the text, highlighting many of the operations that require special attention. Tim Parker advised about the way in which the text should be presented and originated the layout.

Spare parts were supplied by Bryan Goss of Yeovil, who proved very convincingly that parts for the older models can be obtained quickly.

We also wish to thank the Avon Rubber Company Limited for their tyre fitting drawings.

The cover photograph was arranged through the courtesy of Vincent and Jerrom Ltd. Taunton.

About this manual

The author of this manual has the conviction that the only way in which a meaningful and easy to follow text can be written is first to do the work himself, under conditions similar to those found in the average household. As a result, the hands seen in the photographs are those of the author. Even the machines are not new, examples that have covered several thousand miles were selected so that the conditions encountered would be typical of those found by the average owner/rider. Unless specially mentioned and considered essential, service tools have not been used. There is invariably alternative means of loosening or slackening some vital component, when service tools are not available and risk of damage is to be avoided at all costs.

Each of the seven chapters is divided into numbered sections. Within the sections are numbered paragraphs. Cross-reference throughout the manual is quite straightforward and logical. When reference is made, 'See Section 6.10' - it means Section 6, paragraph 10 in the same chapter. If another chapter were meant it would say 'See Chapter 2, Section 6.10'.

All photographs are captioned with a section/paragraph number to which they refer, and are always relevant to the chapter text adjacent.

Figure numbers (usually line illustrations) appear in numerical order, within a given chapter. 'Fig 1.1' therefore refers to the first figure in Chapter 1.

Left hand and right hand descriptions of the machines and their components refer to the left and right of a given machine when normally seated facing the front wheel.

Whilst every care is taken to ensure that the information in this manual is correct no liability can be accepted by the authors or publishers for loss, damage or injury caused by any errors in or omissions from the information given.

Modifications to the Honda 65, 70 and 90 range

Ten years have passed since the small capacity Hondas first reached the UK, a period during which many design changes and detail improvements have been made. Any significant changes are mentioned in the text, under a separate heading where appropriate. It is appreciated that some variants of the models included in this manual were supplied to countries other than the UK but in the main these differences relate to the lighting equipment, which has to meet the statutory requirements of the country into which the machine is imported.

Contents

			Page
Introductory sections		Introduction to the Honda 65, 70 and 90 models	5
		Ordering spare parts	6
		Routine maintenance	7
		Recommended lubricants	9
Chapter One/Engine and gearbox	Part 1 (ohv)	Specifications	11
		Dismantling	13
		Examination and renovation	19
		Reassembly	21
	Part 2 (ohc)	Specifications	31
		Dismantling	34
		Reassembly	38
		Fault diagnosis	46
Chapter Two/Clutch		Specifications	47
		Dismantling	47
		Examination and renovation	49
		Reassembly and adjustment	50
		Fault diagnosis	50
Chapter Three/Fuel system and carburation		Specifications	51
		Carburettor	52
		Exhaust system	54
		Fault diagnosis	56
Chapter Four/Ignition system		Specifications	57
		Contact breaker	57
		Ignition timing	58
		Sparking plug	58
		Fault diagnosis	60
Chapter Five/Frame and fork assembly		Front forks	61
		Steering head	62
		Swinging arm	67
		Speedometer	67
		Cleaning	69
		Fault diagnosis	70
Chapter Six/Wheels, brakes and final drive		Specifications	71
		Front wheel and brake	71
		Rear wheel and brake	75
		Rear chain	78
		Tyres	80
		Fault diagnosis	82
Chapter Seven/Electrical system		Specifications	83
		Battery	83
		Lights	84
		Wiring diagrams	88
Metric conversion table			92
Index			93

Honda 65

Honda 90

Introduction to the Honda 65, 70 and 90 models

During November 1962 Honda introduced into the UK, their range of small capacity motor cycles with an impact that was dramatic in the extreme. Within a very short period of time these models outsold all other machines of similar capacity and Honda became a household word.

In 1964 the first model in the 65 cc - 90 cc range was imported into the UK. This was the C200 model, an 87 cc motor cycle which had an overhead valve engine, manual clutch and a four-speed gearbox. It was supplemented by the model CM90, which was fitted with a similar engine but was constructed along scooter-type lines, with an automatic clutch and a three-speed gearbox.

The overhead valve engine was superceded by a new overhead camshaft design, which provided enhanced performance at the expense of very little increase in petrol consumption. The model CM90 was redesigned using this engine and a new model, the S90, sold alongside and eventually replaced the C200 model. For those who required a smaller capacity machine, which could be used on Britain's Motorways, the model S65 was introduced. The 63 cc overhead camshaft engine provided surprisingly good performance and was above the 50 cc minimum capacity rating in the Motorway Regulations that debarred the smaller capacity models.

Although no specific mention is made of the miniature model ST70 "Monkey Bike", the engine is identical to that of the C70 model, described fully in this Manual.

The C70 and C90 scooter-type variants are currently in production, using the same basic design of overhead camshaft engine - proof enough of the ever-continuing demand for the small capacity Hondas that have established a new trend in motor cycling.

Model dimensions

Wheelbase

S65   1150 mm (46.65 in)
C70   1188 mm (46.7 in)
S90   1195 mm (47.08 in)
C90   1190 mm (46.89 in)
CM90 1186 mm (46.6 in)
C200 1160 mm (47.04 in)

Ground clearance

S65   130 mm (5.12 in)
C70   130 mm (5.12 in)
S90   145 mm (5.71 in)
C90   130 mm (5.12 in)
CM90 150 mm (5.9 in)
C200 135 mm (5.32 in)

Overall length

S65   1795 mm (70.67 in)
C70   1795 mm (70.67 in)
S90   1890 mm (74.74 in)
C90   1830 mm (72.10 in)
CM90 1836 mm (72.30 in)
C200 1805 mm (71.08 in)

Overall width

S65   640 mm (25.19 in)
C70   640 mm (25.19 in)
S90   650 mm (25.61 in)
C90   640 mm (25.19 in)
CM90 570 mm (22.4 in)
C200 625 mm (24.6 in)

Overall height

S65   975 mm (38.4 in)
C70   975 mm (38.4 in)
S90   980 mm (38.61 in)
C90   995 mm (39.20 in)
CM90 964 mm (38.02 in)
C200 955 mm (37.62 in)

Dry weight

S65   69 kg (152 lb)
C70   72 kg (159 lb)
S90   86.5 kg (191 lb)
C90   85 kg (187 lb)
CM90 83 kg (183 lb)
C200 85.5 kg (189 lb)

Ordering spare parts

When ordering spare parts for any of the Honda 65 cc - 90 cc models, it is advisable to deal direct with an official Honda agent, who should be able to supply most items ex-stock. Parts cannot be obtained from Honda (UK) Limited direct; all orders must be routed via an approved agent, even if the parts required are not held in stock.

Always quote the engine and frame numbers in full, particularly if parts are required for any of the earlier models. The frame number is stamped on the left-hand side of the frame, close to the top mounting point of the engine unit. The engine number is stamped on the left-hand crankcase, immediately below the flywheel generator cover.

Use only parts of genuine Honda manufacture. Pattern parts are available, some of which originate from Japan and are packaged to resemble the originals. In many instances these parts will have an adverse effect on performance and/or reliability.

Some of the more expendable parts such as spark plugs, bulbs, tyres, oils and greases etc., can be obtained from accessory shops and motor factors, who have convenient opening hours, charge lower prices and can often be found not far from home. It is also possible to obtain parts on a Mail Order basis from a number of specialists who advertise regularly in the motor cycle magazines.

Frame number plate

Engine number plate

Routine maintenance

Periodic routine maintenance is a continuous process that commences immediately the machine is used. It must be carried out at specified mileage recordings or on a calendar basis if the machine is not used frequently, whichever the soonest. Maintenance should be regarded as an insurance policy, to help keep the machine in the peak of condition and to ensure long, trouble-free service. It has the additional benefit of giving early warning of any faults that may develop and will act as a safety check, to the obvious advantage of both rider and machine alike.

The various maintenance tasks are described below, under their respective mileage and calendar headings. Accompanying diagrams are provided, where necessary. It should be remembered that the interval between the various maintenance tasks serves only as a guide. As the machine gets older or is used under particularly adverse conditions, it would be advisable to reduce the period between each check.

Some of the tasks are described in detail, where they are not mentioned fully as a routine maintenance item in the text. If a specific item is mentioned but not described in detail, it will be covered fully in the appropriate Chapter. No special tools are required for the normal routine maintenance tasks. The tools contained in the tool kit supplied with every new machine will prove adequate for each task, but if they are not available, the tools found in the average household should suffice.

Weekly, or every 200 miles

Check the sump oil level and top up if necessary. Always place the machine on level ground, using the centre stand. If the engine is warm, allow at least five minutes for the oil level to settle, before checking. The dipstick is located on the right-hand side of the engine, at the rear of the crankcase casting. It has an integral cap and screws into the casting, to seal off the oil filler opening. Remove the dipstick and add oil until the upper level mark of the dipstick is reached. For checking purposes, the dipstick should be rested on the edge of the filler opening and not screwed home.

Check the tyre pressures. Always check with the tyres cold, using a pressure gauge known to be accurate.

Check the level of the electrolyte in the battery. Use only distilled water to top up, unless there has been a spillage of acid. Do not overfill. Give the whole machine a close visual inspection, checking for loose nuts and fittings, frayed control cables etc. Make sure the lights, horn and traffic indicators function correctly.

Monthly, or every 1,000 miles

Complete all the checks listed in the weekly/200 mile service, and the following item:

Change the engine oil. Drain off the old oil whilst the engine is still warm to ensure complete and rapid draining. Just over a pint will be released. If the machine is used for a succession of short journeys, it is preferable to halve the period between oil changes, to offset the effects of condensation.

Six Monthly, or every 3,000 miles

Complete all the checks under the weekly and monthly headings, then carry out the following additional tasks:

Check valve tappet clearances and adjust if necessary.

Check and adjust (or replace) the sparking plug.
Check the ignition timing and adjust if necessary.

Clean the air filter element.
Check throttle for correct amount of free play.
Check fuel tap gauze and clean if necessary.
Check fuel tank and fuel lines for leaks, air locks and sediment.
Check clutch operation and adjust if necessary.
Adjust and lubricate final drive chain. If worn, replace in conjunction with sprockets.
Check action of both brakes and adjust if necessary.

Examine both wheels for dented or buckled rims and loose spokes. Check tread on both tyres. If uneven wear has taken place or if the tread depth is close to the statutory minimum replace as a matter of urgency.

Apply a grease gun to all grease nipples and continue pumping action until clean grease emerges from joints.

Check condition of return spring on centre stand.

Check horn and speedometer for correct functioning, bearing in mind that the efficient operation of the former is a statutory requirement.

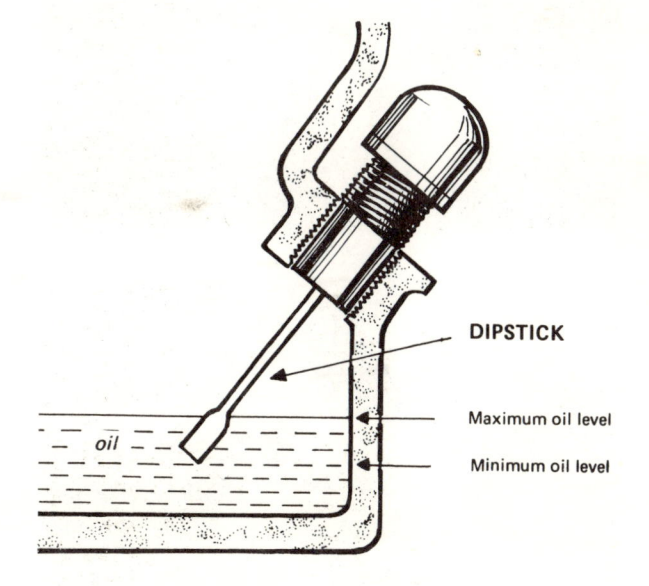

Fig RM1 Crankcase dipstick

Routine Maintenance

Yearly, or every 6,000 miles

Again complete all the checks listed under the weekly, monthly and six monthly headings, but only if they are not directly connected with the tasks listed below. Then complete the following:

Change the engine oil. When the old oil has drained off, remove the right-hand crankcase cover and clean the oil filter screen by washing with petrol. (In the case of the C200 and early CM90 models, the filter assembly is bolted to the base of the right-hand crankcase - there is no necessity to remove the right-hand crankcase cover to gain access).

Remove the air filter and fit a new replacement.

Remove both wheels and check condition of front and rear brake shoes. Replace if linings are thin.

Check steering head bearings for slackness, with machine on centre stand. Do not overtighten.

Check operation of steering head lock.

Fig RM2 Oiling clutch and front brake levers

Fig RM3 Releasing twist grip cover

Fig RM4 Apply grease to slider

Fig RM5 Greasing fork bottom link pivots

Fig RM6 Greasing fork damper pivots

Fig RM7 Oiling rear brake adjuster

Fig RM8 Don't forget the seat catch

Specifications

Lubrication system capacity (engine and gearbox in unit)	0.9 litres (1.90 Imperial pints) (1.58 U.S. pints)
Recommended lubricants	Below 0°C (32°F) SAE 10W 0°C–15°C (32°F–59°F) SAE 20W Over 15°C (59°F) SAE 30
Tappet clearance (engine cold)	0.002 inch inlet and exhaust
Contact breaker gap	0.014 inch
Sparking plug gap	0.024 - 0.028 inch
Tyre pressures - C200	24 psi front, 30 psi rear
- CM90	21 psi front, 25 psi rear
- C90	21 psi front, 25 psi rear
- S90	21 psi front, 25 psi rear
- C70	23 psi front, 28 psi rear
- S65	23 psi front, 28 psi rear

Increase rear tyre pressure by approximately 4 psi when a pillion passenger is carried

Recommended lubricants

COMPONENT	TYPE OF LUBRICANT	CORRECT CASTROL PRODUCTS

ENGINE
   Normal temperatures
   Below freezing point
	Multi-grade 20W/50 to API SE Specification
	
	Multigrade 10W/30
		CASTROL GTX
		
		CASTROLITE

FINAL DRIVE CHAIN	Multigrade engine oil or graphited grease	CASTROL GTX CASTROL GRAPHITED GREASE
ALL GREASING POINTS	Multi-purpose high melting point lithium-based grease	CASTROL LM GREASE

The engine oil should be changed every 1,000 miles. In winter, or when the machine is used for short journeys only, the oil must be changed every 300 miles

Castrol GRADES

Castrol Engine Oils

Castrol GTX

An ultra high performance SAE 20W/50 motor oil which exceeds the latest API MS requirements and manufacturers' specifications. Castrol GTX with liquid tungsten† generously protects engines at the extreme limits of performance, and combines both good cold starting with oil consumption control. Approved by leading car makers.

Castrol XL 20/50

Contains liquid tungsten†; well suited to the majority of conditions giving good oil consumption control in both new and old cars.

Castrolite (Multi-grade)

This is the lightest multi-grade oil of the Castrol motor oil family containing liquid tungsten†. It is best suited to ensure easy winter starting and for those car models whose manufacturers specify lighter weight oils.

Castrol Grand Prix

An SAE 50 engine oil for use where a heavy, full-bodied lubricant is required.

Castrol Two-Stroke-Four

A premium SAE 30 motor oil possessing good detergency characteristics and corrosion inhibitors, coupled with low ash forming tendency and excellent anti-scuff properties. It is suitable for all two-stroke motor-cycles, and for two-stroke and small four-stroke horticultural machines.

Castrol CR (Multi-grade)

A high quality engine oil of the SAE-20W/30 multi-grade type, suited to mixed fleet operations.

Castrol CRI 10, 20, 30

Primarily for diesel engines, a range of heavily fortified, fully detergent oils, covering the requirements of DEF 2101-D and Supplement 1 specifications.

Castrol CRB 20, 30

Primarily for diesel engines, heavily fortified, fully detergent oils, covering the requirements of MIL-L-2104B.

Castrol R 40

Primarily designed and developed for highly stressed racing engines. Castrol 'R' should not be mixed with any other oil nor with any grade of Castrol.

†*Liquid Tungsten is an oil soluble long chain tertiary alkyl primary amine tungstate covered by British Patent No. 882,295.*

Castrol Gear Oils

Castrol Hypoy (90 EP)

A light-bodied powerful extreme pressure gear oil for use in hypoid rear axles and in some gearboxes.

Castrol Gear Oils (continued)

Castrol Hypoy Light (80 EP)

A very light-bodied powerful extreme pressure gear oil for use in hypoid rear axles in cold climates and in some gearboxes.

Castrol Hypoy B (90 EP)

A light-bodied powerful extreme pressure gear oil that complies with the requirements of the MIL-L-2105B specification, for use in certain gearboxes and rear axles.

Castrol Hi-Press (140 EP)

A heavy-bodied extreme pressure gear oil for use in spiral bevel rear axles and some gearboxes.

Castrol ST (90)

A light-bodied gear oil with fortifying additives

Castrol D (140)

A heavy full-bodied gear oil with fortifying additives.

Castrol Thio-Hypoy FD (90 EP)

A light-bodied powerful extreme pressure gear oil. This is a special oil for running-in certain hypoid gears.

Automatic Transmission Fluids

Castrol TQF

(Automatic Transmission Fluid)

Approved for use in all Borg-Warner Automatic Transmission Units. Castrol TQF also meets Ford specification M2C 33F.

Castrol TQ Dexron®

(Automatic Transmission Fluid)

Complies with the requirements of Dexron® Automatic Transmission Fluids as laid down by General Motors Corporation.

Castrol Greases

Castrol LM

A multi-purpose high melting point lithium based grease approved for most automotive applications including chassis and wheel bearing lubrication.

Castrol MS3

A high melting point lithium based grease containing molybdenum disulphide.

Castrol BNS

A high melting point grease for use where recommended by certain manufacturers in front wheel bearings when disc brakes are fitted.

Castrol Greases (continued)

Castrol CL

A semi-fluid calcium based grease, which is both waterproof and adhesive, intended for chassis lubrication.

Castrol Medium

A medium consistency calcium based grease.

Castrol Heavy

A heavy consistency calcium based grease.

Castrol PH

A white grease for plunger housings and other moving parts on brake mechanisms. *It must NOT be allowed to come into contact with brake fluid when applied to the moving parts of hydraulic brakes.*

Castrol Graphited Grease

A graphited grease for the lubrication of transmission chains.

Castrol Under-Water Grease

A grease for the under-water gears of outboard motors.

Anti-Freeze

Castrol Anti-Freeze

Contains anti-corrosion additives with ethylene glycol. Recommended for the cooling systems of all petrol and diesel engines.

Speciality Products

Castrol Girling Damper Oil Thin

The oil for Girling piston type hydraulic dampers.

Castrol Shockol

A light viscosity oil for use in some piston type shock absorbers and in some hydraulic systems employing synthetic rubber seals. It must not be used in braking systems.

Castrol Penetrating Oil

A leaf spring lubricant possessing a high degree of penetration and providing protection against rust.

Castrol Solvent Flushing Oil

A light-bodied solvent oil, designed for flushing engines, rear axles, gearboxes and gearcasings.

Castrollo

An upper cylinder lubricant for use in the proportion of 1 fluid ounce to two gallons of fuel.

Everyman Oil

A light-bodied machine oil containing anti-corrosion additives for both general use and cycle lubrication.

Chapter 1 Engine and Gearbox (ohv type) Part 1

Contents

General description ... 1	Camshaft pinion, camshaft and cam followers - examination 24
Operations with engine/gearbox in frame ... 2	Timing pinions - examination ... 25
Operations with engine/gearbox removed ... 3	Gearbox components - examination ... 26
Method of engine/gearbox removal ... 4	Engine reassembly - general ... 27
Removing the engine/gearbox unit ... 5	Engine reassembly - fitting bearings to crankcases ... 28
Dismantling the engine and gearbox - general .. 6	Engine reassembly - left-hand crankcase ... 29
Dismantling the engine and gearbox - removal of generator ... 7	Engine reassembly - fitting the kickstarter shaft assembly ... 30
Rocker box, cylinder head and cylinder - removal ... 8	Engine reassembly - fitting the crankshaft assembly ... 31
Piston and piston rings - removal ... 9	Engine reassembly - fitting the piston and cylinder barrel ... 32
Valves and rockers - removal ... 10	Engine reassembly - replacing camshaft and camshaft pinion ... 33
Crankcases - separating ... 11	Engine reassembly - fitting gear change assembly ... 34
Crankshaft assembly - removal ... 12	Engine reassembly - fitting and tensioning kickstarter return spring ... 35
Kickstarter shaft and ratchet assembly - removal ... 13	Engine reassembly - locating the driver gear and clutch assembly ... 36
Gear selector drum and gear cluster - removal.. 14	Engine reassembly - fitting a.c. generator ... 37
Oil seals - removal ... 15	Engine reassembly - setting the contact breaker points ... 38
Crankshaft and gearbox main bearings - removal ... 16	Engine reassembly - checking and resetting the ignition timing ... 39
Examination and renovation - general ... 17	Engine reassembly - fitting the cylinder head and rocker box 40
Big-end and main bearings - examination and renovation ... 18	Engine reassembly - adjusting the tappets ... 41
Cylinder barrel - examination and renovation ... 19	Engine reassembly - completion and final adjustments ... 42
Piston and piston rings - examination and renovation ... 20	Refitting the engine/gearbox unit in frame ... 43
Valves, valve seats and valve guides - examination and renovation.. ... 21	Starting and running the rebuilt engine ... 44
Cylinder head - decarbonisation and examination ... 22	
Rockers and rocker shafts - examination ... 23	

The Honda 90 cc models included in this manual have been fitted with two types of engine, an overhead valve and an overhead camshaft design. Both are dealt with in this Chapter but in two separate parts. Part 1 concerns the ohv engine and Part 2, the ohc engine. The work necessary is described in full in the first part for the ohv engine, but is not repeated in the second part where it is the same, due to basic similarities in design. A fault finding table applicable to both types of engine is given at the conclusion of the Chapter.

Specifications

Engine (ohv type)
Type ... Single cylinder overhead valve, push rod operated
Cylinder head .. Cast iron
Cylinder barrel ... Cast iron
Bore ... 49 mm
Stroke... 46 mm
Capacity ... 86.7 cc
Bhp ... 6.5 @ 7,500 rpm
Compression ratio ... 8 : 1

Piston rings
Compression (two top rings) ... Top ring chrome, second ring tapered
Oil control ring ... Third ring, at top of skirt

Valves
Tappet clearance, inlet and exhaust ... 0.002 inch, set with engine cold
Seat angle ... 45°

Chapter 1/Engine and gearbox (ohv type) Part 1

Capacities
Engine and gearbox (in unit) ... ... 0.9 litres 1.5 Imp. pints
1.90 U.S. pints

Torque wrench settings
Cylinder head nuts ... ... 70 in lb
Rocker oil feed pipe bolts ... ... 60 in lb
Carburettor mounting nuts ... ... 60 in lb

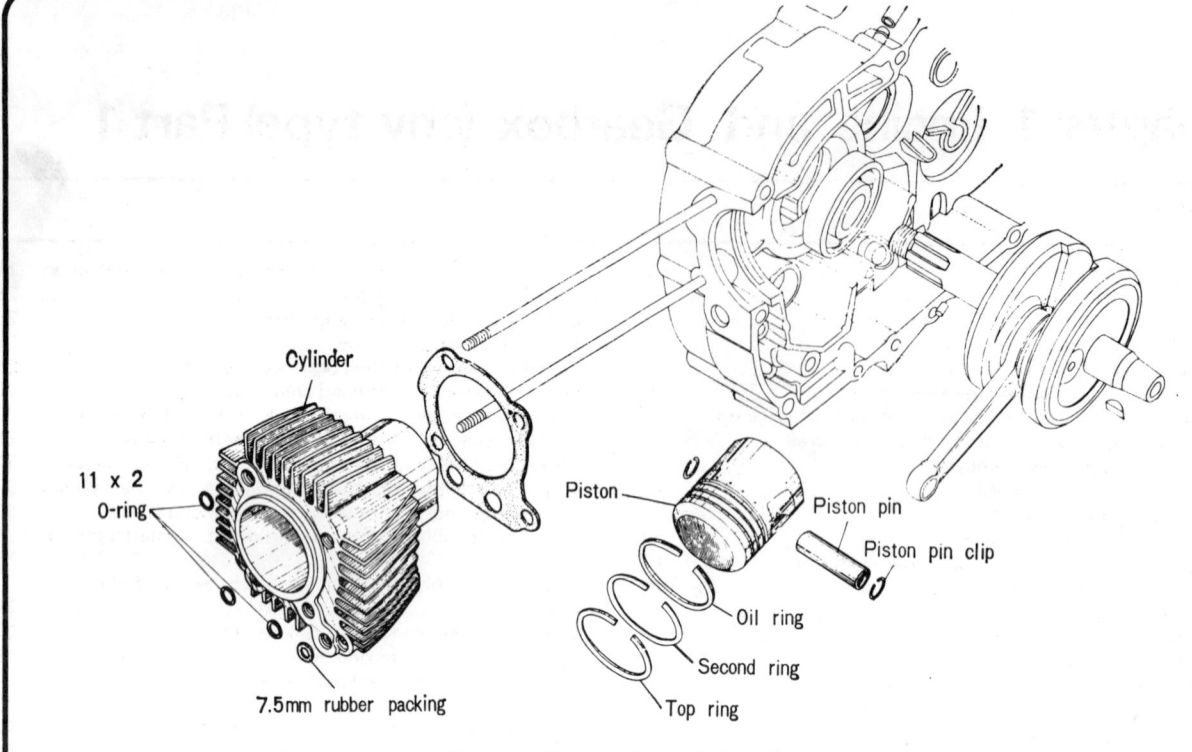

Fig. 1.1A. Piston and cylinder barrel

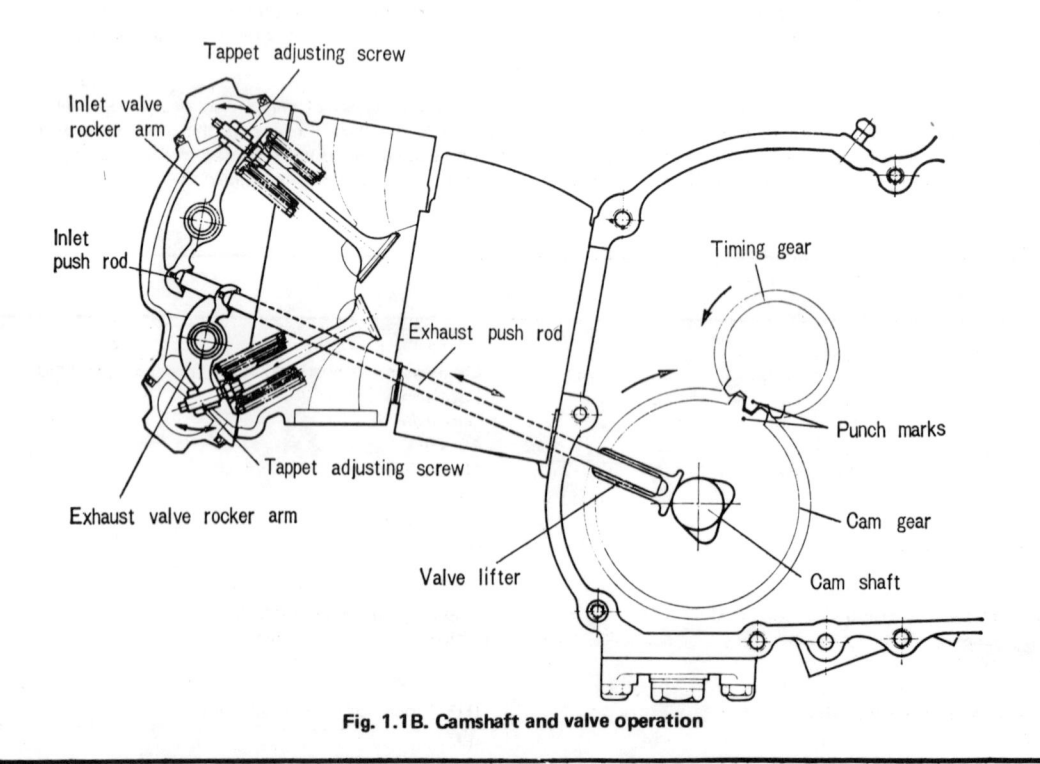

Fig. 1.1B. Camshaft and valve operation

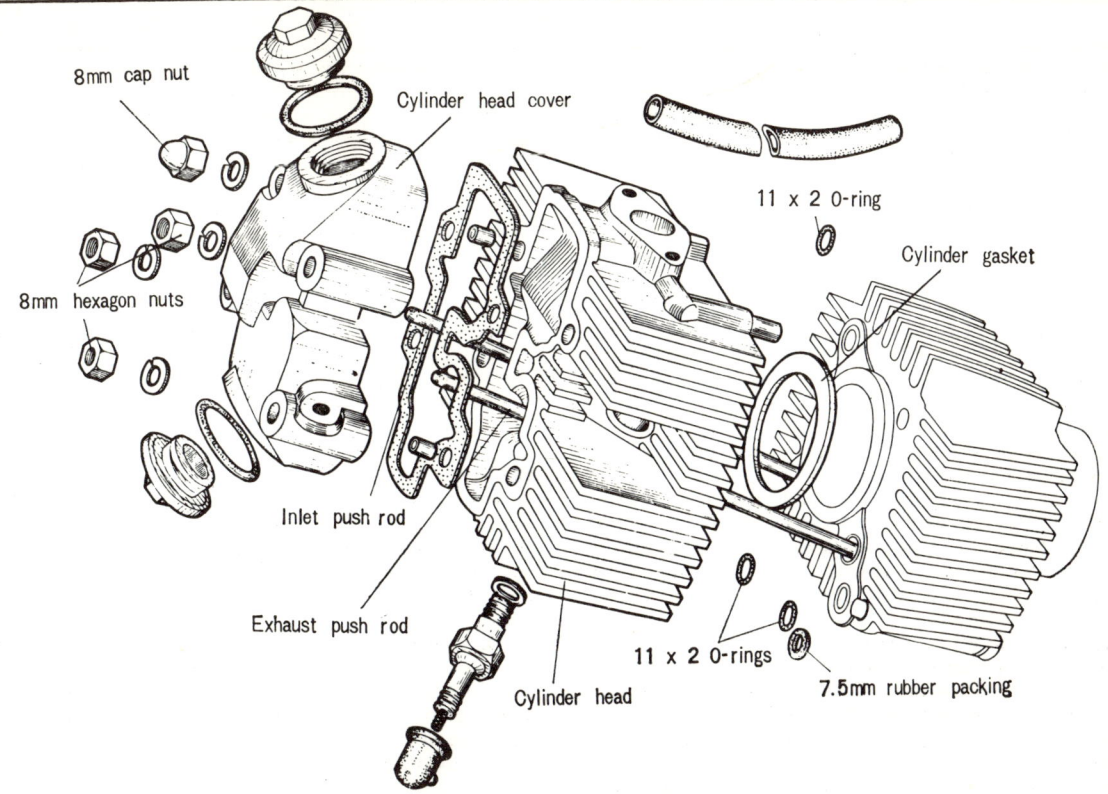

Fig. 1.2. Cylinder head, barrel and rocker cover

1 General description

The engine unit fitted to the Honda C200 and the early CM90 models is of the overhead valve type in which the valve gear is actuated by pushrods. The later CM90, CS90 (S90), C90, C70 and S65 models have an overhead camshaft engine unit, in which the valve mechanism is chain driven. The camshaft itself is located within the cylinder head casting.

All engine/gear units are of aluminium alloy construction, with a cast iron cylinder barrel. The C200 and early CM90 models have also a cast iron cylinder head as distinct from the other models which have this component cast in light alloy. The flywheel generator is mounted on the left-hand side of the engine unit; the clutch assembly is located on the right-hand side of the engine, behind a domed aluminium alloy cover. Convention is defied by installing the engine/gear unit in a near-horizontal position, so that the cylinder barrel is almost parallel to the ground. The exhaust system is carried on the right-hand side of the machine and may be of either the upswept or downswept pattern, depending on the specification of the machine. All models are fitted with a conventional kickstarter.

Both push rod and overhead camshaft engines are lubricated by means of a mechanically-operated oil pump which draws oil from the crankcase sump and feeds it through passages in the left-hand crankcase to the gearbox mainshaft. A second feed is arranged via the gearbox layshaft to the lower part of the right-hand crankcase and crankcase cover. From the crankcase cover, oil passes to the clutch cover, oil filter and crankshaft assembly. Another passage feeds oil to the timing gear, cam gear and primary transmission. One further passage distributes oil to the cylinder, cylinder head and rocker gear before it returns to the crankcase. This arrangement applies specifically to the push rod engines; a somewhat similar route is adopted for the overhead camshaft engines where a positive feed to the camshaft and rocker gear is essential.

Both types of engine are built in unit with the gearbox. This means that when the engine is dismantled, the gearbox has to be dismantled too, and vica-versa.

2 Operations with engine/gearbox in frame

It is not necessary to remove the engine unit from the frame unless the crankshaft assembly and/or the gearbox bearings require attention. Most operations can be accomplished with the engine in place, such as:
1 Removal and replacement of cylinder head.
2 Removal and replacement of cylinder barrel and piston.
3 Removal and replacement of flywheel magnetic generator.
4 Removal and replacement of clutch assembly.
5 Removal and replacement of timing pinions and kickstarter assembly.

When several operations need to be undertaken simultaneously, it will probably be advantageous to remove the complete engine unit from the frame, an operation that should take approximately twenty minutes. This will give the advantage of better access and more working space.

3 Operations with engine/gearbox removed

1 Removal and replacement of the main bearings.
2 Removal and replacement of the crankshaft assembly.
3 Removal and replacement of the gear cluster, selectors and gearbox main bearings.

4 Method of engine/gearbox removal

As described previously, the engine and gearbox are built in unit and it is necessary to remove the unit complete in order to gain access to either component. Separation is accomplished after the engine unit has been removed and refitting cannot take place until the crankcase has been reassembled.

5 Removing the engine/gearbox unit

1 Place the machine on the centre stand and make sure it is standing firmly. Remove the crankcase drain plug and drain oil from the crankcase.
2 Remove air cleaner lid and withdraw element. (10 mm dome nut) (CM90, C90 and C70 models only).
3 Remove the front legshield assembly (held by four 10 mm bolts). Slacken off the legshield rear clamp plates (14 mm nuts) (CM90, C90 and C70 models only).
4 Remove exhaust system complete. (Two 10 mm nuts at cylinder head and two 10 mm bolts retaining silencer to frame bracket).
5 Remove the copper asbestos joint ring from exhaust port.
6 Disconnect battery leads.
7 Remove air filter hose from carburettor.
8 Unscrew top from main body of carburettor and withdraw the throttle slide and needle.
9 Pull off petrol pipe and remove the induction pipe. Remove carburettor. In the case of the C90 and C70 model it will be necessary to block the pipe immediately the carburettor is removed from the cylinder head (two 10 mm nuts), unless the petrol tank is drained. In these models, the petrol tap is integral with the float chamber top.
10 Remove carburettor flange 'O' ring.
11 Remove sparking plug lead by pulling off cap.
12 Disconnect the brown coloured wire from the rectifier and the four generator wires coloured white, yellow, blue and green with red stripe. These wires are fitted with snap connectors that pull apart.
13 Remove the footrest assembly, which is attached to the crankcase by four 14 mm bolts and spring washers. It is possible to remove the engine/gear unit with the footrests in place, if it is desired to use them as a convenient carrying handle.
14 Remove the lower section of the rear chaincase (if fitted) by removing the two 10 mm bolts. Remove also the small forward mounted aluminium alloy sprocket cover (four cross-head screws).
15 Disconnect the rear chain at the connecting link and remove the chain.
16 Remove the small plastic section of the rear chainguard (if fitted).
17 Unhook the brake pedal and stop-lamp switch springs.
18 Place a support under the engine unit and remove the upper and lower engine mounting bolts. The complete engine/gear unit can now be lifted clear of the frame.

6 Dismantling the engine and gearbox - general

Before commencing work on the engine unit, the external surfaces should be cleaned thoroughly. A motor cycle engine has very little protection from road grit and other foreign matter, which will find its way into the dismantled engine if this simple precaution is not observed. One of the proprietary engine cleaning compounds such as 'Gunk' can be used to good effect, particularly if the compound is allowed to work into the film of grease and oil before it is washed away. When washing down, make sure that water cannot enter the carburettor or the electrical system, particularly if these parts have been exposed.

Never use undue force to remove any stubborn part, unless mention is made of this requirement. There is invariable good reason why a part is difficult to remove, often because the dismantling operation has been tackled in the wrong sequence.

Dismantling will be made easier if a simple engine stand is constructed that will correspond with the engine mounting points. This arrangement will permit the complete unit to be clamped rigidly to the work bench, leaving both hands free.

7 Dismantling the engine and gearbox - removal of generator

1 Remove the gear change and kickstarter pedals, which are retained on their splined shafts by a 14 mm pinch bolt. Note the position of each pedal before drawing off the shaft (late models have centre punch marks to aid relocation).
2 Remove the two rocker box inspection caps (17 mm spanner) and the external rocker oil feed pipe (10 mm spanner). The inspection caps are damaged very easily if an incorrect size spanner is used.
3 Remove the gearbox sprocket, which is retained to the gearbox mainshaft by two 10 mm screws and a retaining plate or a centre bolt.
4 Remove flywheel magneto generator cover, which is retained by five cross head screws.

S65 model only:

5 Remove the 14 mm nut and washer retaining the flywheel magneto generator to the crankshaft and pull the flywheel from the crankshaft using either a flywheel extractor that screws into the internal threads of the flywheel centre or a chain pulled tight around the outside of the flywheel and a two-legged puller (see drawing).
6 Disconnect the green/red striped wire from the neutral indicator switch and remove the switch.
7 Remove the two countersunk cross head screws holding the stator plate to the crankcase and remove the stator plate complete with wires.
8 Remove the Woodruff key from the crankshaft.

All other models:

These machines have a different type of generator, which necessitates revised dismantling procedure:
9 Remove the stator plate inspection cover (circular cover on left-hand flywheel generator cover).
10 Remove the complete left-hand crankcase cover that houses the stator assembly. This cover is retained by four cross head screws.
11 Disconnect the green/red striped wire from the neutral indicator contact and remove the complete stator coil assembly from the left-hand crankcase by unscrewing the cross head screws. Remove the neutral indicator contact.
12 Hold the rotor stationary and remove the centre retaining bolt and washer. Lift off the automatic advance and retard mechanism. (C200 and early CM90 models only).
13 Remove the rotor. If the correct service tool extractor is not available, use a sprocket puller bearing on a footrest bolt screwed part way into the end of the crankshaft.

8 Rocker box, cylinder head and cylinder removal

C200 and early CM90 engines only

1 Remove the four 8 mm nuts retaining the rocker box cover and lift it clear of the cylinder head.
2 Lift out the two pushrods. There is no need to mark them because the exhaust pushrod is the shorter of the two.
3 Lift the cylinder head away from the cylinder barrel by sliding it up the studs.
4 The cylinder barrel can now be lifted from the crankcase, leaving the holding down studs that thread direct into the crankcase assembly. Note there is a gasket between the rocker box and the cylinder head, a copper ring-type gasket between the cylinder head and barrel and 'O' ring rubbers to seal the pushrod tunnels and the oil drainaway from the rocker gear. All should be renewed when the engine is reassembled.

5.1. Drain off oil by removing drain plug

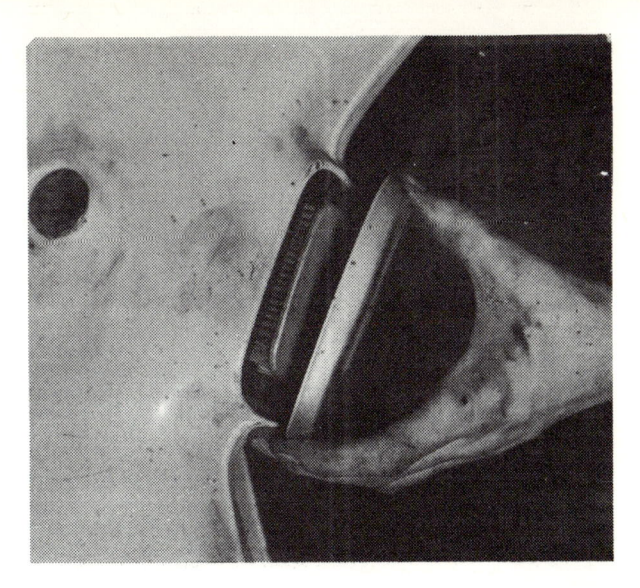

5.2. Remove air cleaner lid

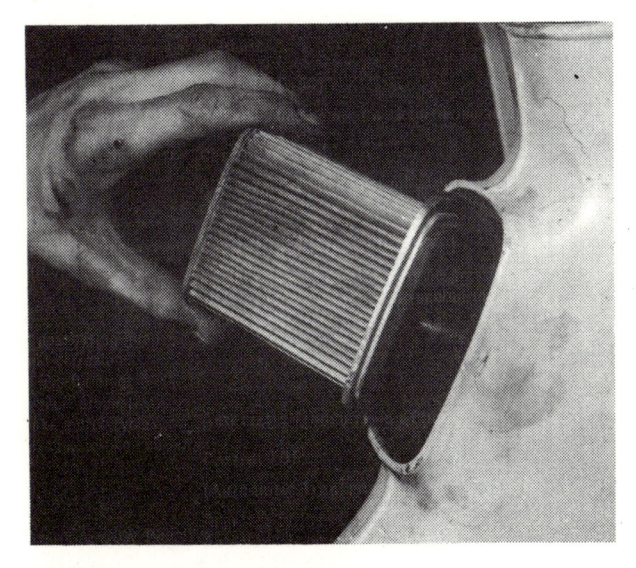

5.2A. Remove air cleaner element

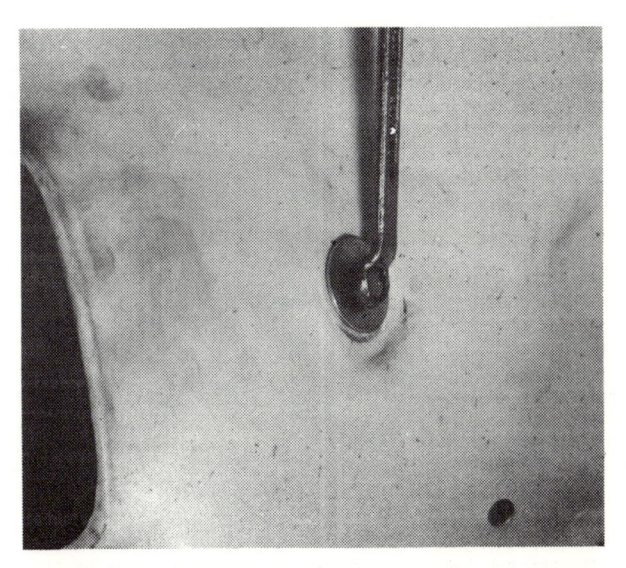

5.3. Remove the legshield retaining bolts

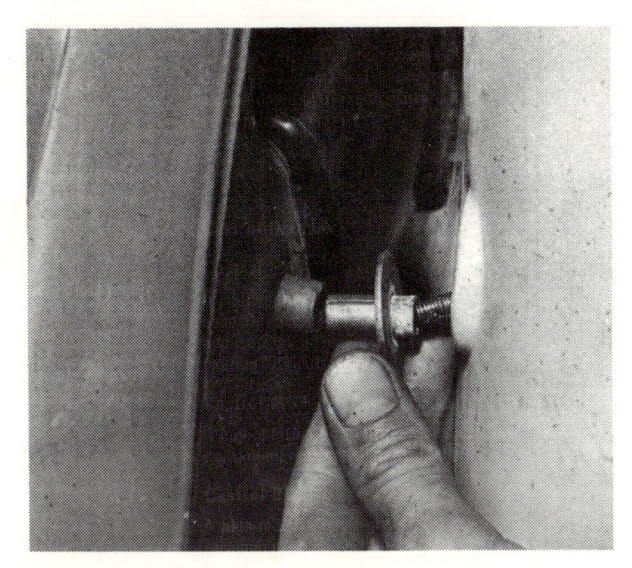

5.3A. Take care not to lose the spacers

5.4. Release exhaust pipe from cylinder head

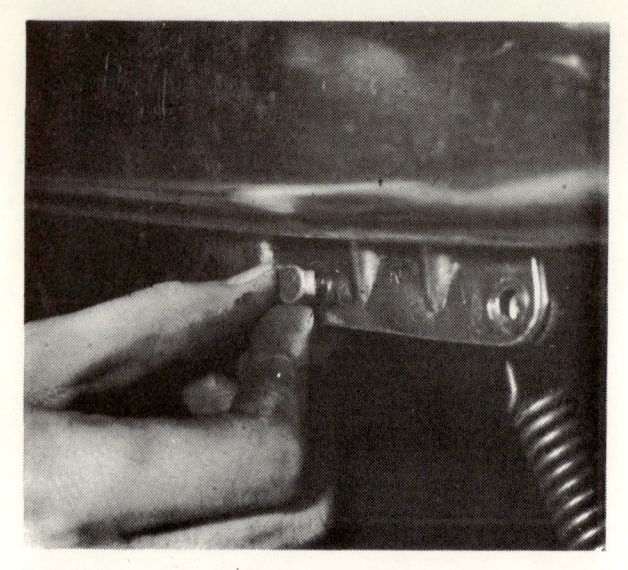

5.4A. Silencer is held to frame by two bolts

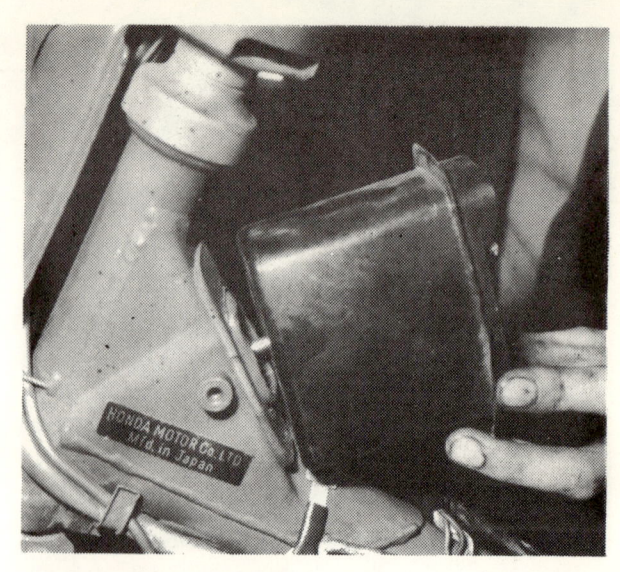

5.6. Withdraw element holder

5.8. Carburettor complete can be removed as alternative

5.12. Snap connectors at rectifier make disconnection easy

5.15. Detach connecting link at rear wheel sprocket

6.3. Removal of locking plate releases sprocket

Chapter 1/Engine and gearbox (ohv type) Part 1

7.9. Lift off stator plate inspection cover

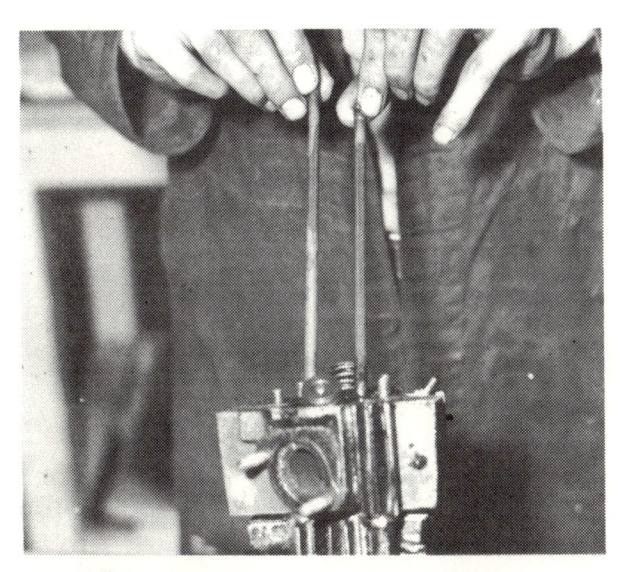

8.2. Withdraw push rods before removing cylinder head

8.4. Cylinder head is released by sliding up holding down studs

9 Piston and piston rings - removal

1 The gudgeon pin is of the fully floating type, retained by two wire circlips in the piston bosses. After the circlips have been removed, using pointed nose pliers, the pin can be tapped lightly from the piston.

2 Note the piston is marked with an arrow and must be positioned so that the arrow points downwards. If the piston is oversize, the amount will be stamped on the piston crown.

3 Remove the piston rings by expanding them gently, using extreme care because they are very brittle. If they prove difficult to remove, slide strips of tin behind them, to help ease them from their grooves. The top piston ring is of the chrome type and should have the mark 'top' on the uppermost face. The second ring is tapered and should have the 'top' mark in a similar position. A slotted oil scraper ring is fitted in the lower groove, which can be located with either face uppermost.

10 Valves and rockers - removal

C200 and early CM90 engines only

1 Use a small size valve spring compressor to compress the springs and release the split-type collets. The valves cannot be interchanged because the inlet valve has a larger head.

2 Remove the two 14 mm plugs from the rocker box shell. The rocker spindles can be pulled out after these caps have been removed by applying pressure with a piece of stiff wire passed down the centre of each spindle. A small compression spring is located between the end of each rocker and the rocker box shell, to take up side play.

11 Crankcases - separating

CM90, C90 and C70 models only:

Before the crankcases can be separated, it is necessary to remove the clutch assembly, primary drive pinions, camshaft pinion (early CM90 models only) and part of the kickstarter and gear change mechanism. Proceed as follows:

1 Remove the clutch cover on the right-hand side of the engine unit. This is retained by nine cross head screws. Note the use of a sealing gasket.

2 When the cover has been removed, it is probable that an anti-rattle spring will have dropped out of position. This is located between the clutch operating cam plate and the release mechanism, to eliminate chatter. Remove the clutch operating lever and washer from its splined shaft, lift off the cam plate, and prise free the ball bearing and carrier from the clutch centre.

3 Remove clutch outer plate by unscrewing the two cross head screws.

4 The complete clutch assembly is splined to the crankshaft and is retained by a sleeve nut and tab washer. Bend back the tab washer and unscrew the sleeve nut, using a special tool made from a short length of conduit, if the appropriate service tool is not available. (See drawing). The complete clutch assembly can then be withdrawn from the shaft.

5 Remove the 17 mm circlip from the gearbox mainshaft. Withdraw the driving pinion.

6 Remove the 23 mm circlip and washer from the kickstarter shaft and disconnect and remove the kickstarter return spring, using pointed nose pliers.

7 Pull out the camshaft pinion, complete with camshaft and withdraw the cam followers, marking them to ensure their correct order of replacement.

8 Remove the crankshaft pinion. In the case of the early CM90 models, this is a tight fit on the crankshaft and is provided with two tapped holes through which two 10 mm bolts can be threaded to act as extractors. Tighten each in turn a small amount, so that the pinion is drawn off the crankshaft gradually. Do not use excessive force or the bolts will shear. If the pinion is a particularly tight fit, the application of local heat will help. All

9.2. Arrow on piston crown ensures correct fitting

10.1. Adaptation of spring compressor with distance piece and washer

10.2. Springs take up rocker end float

11.5. Removal of circlip releases driving pinion

11.7. Camshaft pinion and camshaft will pull out of crankcase

Clutch sleeve tool
1. Holes for tommy bar
2. Two pegs to engage with sleeve nut
3. Sleeve nut

other models use a different arrangement where the pinion and its internal bush are a sliding fit on the crankshaft.

9 Slacken off the 10 mm bolt which locates the gear indexing pawl, to permit the pawl to be disengaged from the selector drum.

10 Depress the gear change lever by hand until it is clear of the selector drum with which it registers. Gently tap the gear change lever spindle out of the crankcase from the left-hand side, taking great care that the mechanism is not stressed.

11 Remove the nine crankcase cross head screws and hold the crankcase assembly over the work bench with the right-hand side uppermost. Gently tap the end of the gearbox mainshaft, the kickstarter shaft and the crankshaft alternately in order, using a rawhide mallet. This will separate the crankcases, leaving the complete gear cluster kickstarter assembly and crankshaft in the left-hand case.

12 Remove the crankcase gasket and the two locating dowels.

C200, S90 and S65 models:
1 Remove the clutch cover as CM90 etc. models.
2 Remove the clutch operating pushrod to which is attached a lubrication reservoir. The trough is attached to an arm that locates in the hollow centre of the gearbox mainshaft. Prise out the ball bearing and bearing carrier from the clutch centre. Later

models have a clutch thrust pad in place of the pushrod and lubricating trough.
3 Remove the clutch outer plate by unscrewing the two cross head screws.
4 Remove the clutch assembly complete, followed by the instructions for the CM90 etc. models.
5 Remove the driving pinion, camshaft drive pinion and camshaft, crankshaft pinion and kickstarter spring. Disengage the gear index mechanism, following the instructions for the CM90 etc. models. The crankcases can now be separated.
6 Note that it will be more difficult to extract the crankshaft timing pinion fitted to the C200 model.

12 Crankshaft assembly - removal

1 The crankcase bearings are a sliding fit in the steel-inserted housings in the crankcase. The crankshaft assembly complete with bearings should withdraw from the left-hand case without difficulty, using only light pressure.

13 Kickstarter shaft and ratchet assembly - removal

1 The complete kickstarter shaft and ratchet assembly can be withdrawn from the left-hand crankcase as a complete assembly. It can then be dismantled in the following order of component parts:
12 mm thrust washer
Kickstarter pinion
14 mm thrust washer
Pawl-lifting camplate
Circlip and pawl spring washer
Pawl spring
Pawl
Large distance washer
2 If it is necessary to remove the carrier for the camplate and pawl from the shaft, the position of the carrier in relation to the milled slot in the shaft should be noted. Both parts are punched marked to aid correct realignment.

14 Gear selector drum and gear cluster - removal

1 Remove the rubber blanking plug located at the side of the neutral indicator switch.
2 Remove the 10 mm bolt and washer retaining the gear selector drum in the crankcase (situated adjacent to the neutral indicator contact. The selector drum can now be withdrawn from the crankcase, together with the selectors and the gear cluster complete. The gear cluster can be dismantled in the following sequence:

CM90, C90 and C70 models:
Three-speed gearbox
Mainshaft assembly   Thrust washer, top gear pinion, splined thrust washer, second gear pinion (integral with mainshaft) and thrust washer.
Layshaft assembly   Thrust washer, top gear pinion, distance piece, second gear pinion, splined thrust washer, circlip, sliding dog, circlip, thrust washer and first gear pinion.
The gear selector forks are positioned on the selector drum by 10 mm screwed pins and tab washers. The neutral indicator contact is attached to the end of the selector drum.

C200, S90 and S65 models:
Four speed gearbox.
Mainshaft assembly   Thrust washer, top gear pinion, splined thrust washer, circlip, third gear pinion and dog combined, circlip, splined thrust washer, second gear pinion, first gear pinion (integral with mainshaft) and thrust washer.
Layshaft assembly   Thrust washer, top gear pinion, distance piece, third gear pinion, splined thrust washer, circlip, second gear pinion and dog combined, circlip, thrust washer and first gear pinion.

14.2. Four speed gear cluster assembly

15 Oil seals - removal

1 Three oil seals are fitted in the left-hand crankcase, located at the crankshaft bearing, gearbox layshaft bearing and gear lever shaft. There is also an oil seal on the kickstarter shaft bearing in the clutch cover.
2 The oil seals are easily removed by prising them out of position with a screwdriver. Care should be taken to ensure the lip of the bearing housing is not damaged during this operation.

16 Crankshaft and gearbox main bearings - removal

1 The crankshaft bearings will remain on their shafts when the crankshaft assembly is withdrawn from the crankcase. A puller or an extractor will be necessary for their removal as they are a tight fit on the shafts.
2 The gearbox bearings are a light press fit in the crankcase castings. They can be drifted out of position, using a mandrel of the correct size and a hammer.
3 If necessary, warm the crankcases slightly, to aid the release of the bearings.

17 Examination and renovation - general

1 Before examining the parts of the dismantled engine unit for wear, it is essential that they should be cleaned thoroughly. Use a paraffin/petrol mix to remove all traces of old oil and sludge that may have accumulated within the engine.
2 Examine the crankcase castings for cracks or other signs of damage. If a crack is discovered, it will require professional repair.
3 Examine carefully each part to determine the extent of wear, if necessary checking with the tolerance figures listed in the Specifications section of this Chapter.
4 Use a clean, lint-free rag for cleaning and drying the various components, otherwise there is risk of small particles obstructing the internal oilways.

18 Big-end and main bearings - examination and renovation

1 Failure of the big-end bearing is invariably accompanied by a knock from within the crankcase that progressively becomes worse. Some vibration will also be experienced. There should be no vertical play in the big-end bearing after the old oil has been washed out. If even a small amount of play is evident, the bearing is due for replacement. Do not run the machine with a

worn big-end bearing, otherwise there is risk of breaking the connecting rod or crankshaft.

2   It is not possible to separate the flywheel assembly in order to replace the bearing because the parallel sided crankpin is pressed into the flywheels. Big-end repair should be entrusted to a Honda agent, who will have the necessary repair or replacement facilities.

3   Failure of the main bearings is usually evident in the form of an audible rumble from the bottom end of the engine, accompanied by vibration. The vibration will be most noticeable through the footrests.

4   The crankshaft main bearings are of the journal ball type. If wear is evident in the form of play or if the bearings feel rough as they are rotated, replacement is necessary. To remove the main bearings if the appropriate service tool is not available, insert two thin steel wedges, one on each side of the bearing, and with these clamped in a vice hit the end of the crankshaft squarely with a rawhide mallet in an attempt to drive the crankshaft through the bearing. When the bearing has moved the initial amount, it should be possible to insert a conventional two or three legged sprocket puller, to complete the drawing-off action.

5   Note that in the case of the overhead camshaft engines, the bottom camshaft chain sprocket must be withdrawn from the left-hand crankshaft before access can be gained to the main bearing. The sprocket is recessed to accommodate a puller.

19 Cylinder barrel - examination and renovation

1   The usual indications of a badly worn cylinder barrel and piston are excessive oil consumption and piston slap, a metallic rattle that occurs when there is little or no load on the engine. If the top of the bore of the cylinder barrel is examined carefully, it will be found that there is a ridge on the thrust side, the depth of which will vary according to the amount of wear that has taken place. This marks the limit of travel of the uppermost piston ring.

2   Measure the bore diameter just below the ridge, using an internal micrometer. Compare this reading with the diameter at the bottom of the cylinder bore, which has not been subject to wear. If the difference in readings exceeds 0.005 inch it is necessary to have the cylinder rebored and to fit an oversize piston and rings.

3   If an internal micrometer is not available, the amount of cylinder bore wear can be measured by inserting the piston without rings so that it is approximately ¾ inch from the top of the bore. If it is possible to insert a 0.004 inch feeler gauge between the piston and the cylinder wall on the thrust side of the piston, remedial action must be taken.

4   Check the surface of the cylinder bore for score marks or any other damage that may have resulted from an earlier engine seizure or displacement of the gudgeon pin. A rebore will be necessary to remove any deep indentations, irrespective of the amount of bore wear, otherwise a compression leak will occur.

5   Check the external cooling fins are not clogged with oil or road dirt; otherwise the engine will overheat. When clean, a coating of matt cylinder black will help improve the heat radiation.

20 Piston and piston rings - examination and renovation

1   If a rebore is necessary, the existing piston and rings can be disregarded because they will be replaced with their oversize equivalents as a matter of course.

2   Remove all traces of carbon from the piston crown, using a soft scraper to ensure the surface is not marked. Finish off by polishing the crown, with metal polish, so that carbon does not adhere so easily in the future. Never use emery cloth.

3   Piston wear usually occurs at the skirt or lower end of the piston and takes the form of vertical streaks or score marks on the thrust side. There may also be some variation in the thickness of the skirt.

4   The piston ring grooves may also become enlarged in use, allowing the piston rings to have greater side float. If the clearance exceeds 0.004 inch for the two compression rings, or 0.005 inch for the oil control ring the piston is due for replacement. It is unusual for this amount of wear to occur on its own.

5   Piston ring wear is measured by removing the rings from the piston and inserting them in the cylinder bore using the crown of the piston to locate them approximately 1½ inches from the top of the bore. Make sure they rest square with the bore. Measure the end gap with a feeler gauge; if the gap exceeds 0.010 inch they require replacement.

21 Valves, valve seats and valve guides - examination and renovation

1   After cleaning the valves to remove all traces of carbon, examine the heads for signs of pitting and burning. Examine also the valve seats in the cylinder head. The exhaust valve and its seat will probably require the most attention because these are the hotter running of the two. If the pitting is slight, the marks can be removed by grinding the seats and valves together, using fine valve grinding compound.

2   Valve grinding is a simple task, carried out as follows: Smear a trace of fine valve grinding compound (carborundum paste) on the seat face and apply a suction grinding tool to the head of the valve. With a semi-rotary motion, grind in the valve head to its seat, using a backward and forward action. It is advisable to lift the valve occasionally, to distribute the grinding compound evenly. Repeat this operation until an unbroken ring of light grey matt finish is obtained on both valve and seat. This denotes the grinding operation is complete. Before passing to the next operation, make quite sure that all traces of the grinding compound have been removed from both the valve and its seat and that none has entered the valve guide. If this precaution is not observed, rapid wear will take place, due to the abrasive nature of the carborundum base.

3   When deeper pit marks are encountered, it will be necessary to use a valve refacing machine and also a valve seat cutter, set to an angle of 45°. Never resort to excessive grinding because this will only pocket the valve and lead to reduced engine efficiency. If there is any doubt about the condition of a valve, fit a new replacement.

4   Examine the condition of the valve collets and the groove on the valve in which they seat. If there is any sign of damage, new replacements should be fitted. If the collets work loose whilst the engine is running, a valve will drop in and cause extensive damage.

5   Measure the valve stems for wear, making reference to the tolerance values given in the Specifications section of this Chapter. Check also the valve guides. If wear is evident, the cylinder head will need to be replaced if it is of the cast iron type. In these cylinder heads, the valve guides are an integral part and cannot be replaced. Alloy cylinder heads are fitted with detachable valve guides, which can be removed by heating the cylinder head in an oven then using a two diameter drift to drive them out of position. The initial diameter of the drift must be a good fit in the valve guide stem. Replace with the new valve guides whilst the cylinder head is still warm.

6   Check the free length of the valve springs against the list of tolerances in the Specifications. If the springs are reduced in length or if there is any doubt about their condition, they should be replaced.

22 Cylinder head - decarbonisation and examination

1   Remove all traces of carbon from the cylinder head and valve ports, using a soft scraper. Extreme care should be taken to ensure the combustion chamber and valve seats are not marked in any way, otherwise hot spots and leakages may occur. Finish by polishing the combustion chamber so that carbon does not adhere so easily in the future. Use metal polish and NOT emery cloth.

2 Check to make sure the valve guides are free from carbon or any other foreign matter that may cause the valves to stick.
3 Make sure the cylinder head fins are not clogged with oil or road dirt, otherwise the engine will overheat. If necessary, use a wire brush. When the fins and outer surfaces are clean, a coating of matt cylinder black will help improve the heat radiation.
4 Reassemble the valves, using a valve spring compressor to compress the springs. Make sure the valve stems have a coating of oil before they are replaced in the valve guides. Also check that the split collets are located positively before the spring compressor is released. A misplaced collet can cause a valve to drop in whilst the engine is running and cause serious damage.

23 Rockers and rocker shafts - examination

1 It is unlikely that excessive wear will occur in the rockers and rocker shafts unless the flow of oil has been impeded or the machine has covered a very large mileage. A clicking noise from the rocker box is the usual symptom of wear in the rocker components, which should not be confused with the noise that results from excessive tappet clearances.
2 If any shake is present and the rocker arm is loose on its shaft, a new rocker and/or shaft should be fitted.
3 Check the tip of the rocker arm at the point where it bears on the end of the pushrod (C200 and early CM90 models) or on the overhead camshaft (late CM90, C90, S90, C70 and S65 models). If signs of cracking, scuffing or break through in the case-hardened surface, fit a new replacement. Check also the condition of the thread on both the tappet and the rocker arm, and the locknut.
4 Check the pushrods for straightness by rolling them on a flat surface. If they are bent, this is often a sign that the engine has been over-revved on some previous occasion. It is better to fit replacements than attempt to straighten the originals. (C200 and early CM90 models only).

24 Camshaft pinion, camshaft and cam followers - examination

(C200 and early CM90 models only:

1 Examine the camshaft pinion for worn or broken teeth, an unusual occurrence that can be attributed to the presence of foreign bodies, or pieces from some other broken engine component.
2 The cams should have a smooth surface and be free from scuff marks or indentations. It is unlikely that severe wear will be encountered during the normal service life of the machine unless the lubrication system has failed or the case hardened surface has broken through.
3 Similar advice applies to the cam followers. They are designed to revolve whilst the engine is running to even out any wear that may take place. Replace only if the base is indented or if there is evidence of wear such as scuffing.
4 Check the oil groove on the end of the camshaft to ensure it is clean and free from sludge. The external oil feed to the rocker box assembly is dependent on the flow of oil from the end of the camshaft. Check also that the external oil feed pipe and the hollow bolts that pass through the unions are clean and free from obstructions.

Late CM90, C90 S90, C70 and S65 models:

1 The use of an overhead camshaft in the engine fitted to these models obviates the need for pushrods, cam followers and a camshaft pinion. The camshaft is driven by a chain and sprocket arrangement; the rocker arms bear direct on the camshaft without any intermediary.
2 Examine the cams and camshaft as in the preceding section relating to the C200 models etc. A spiral groove in both ends of the camshaft forms part of the lubrication system.

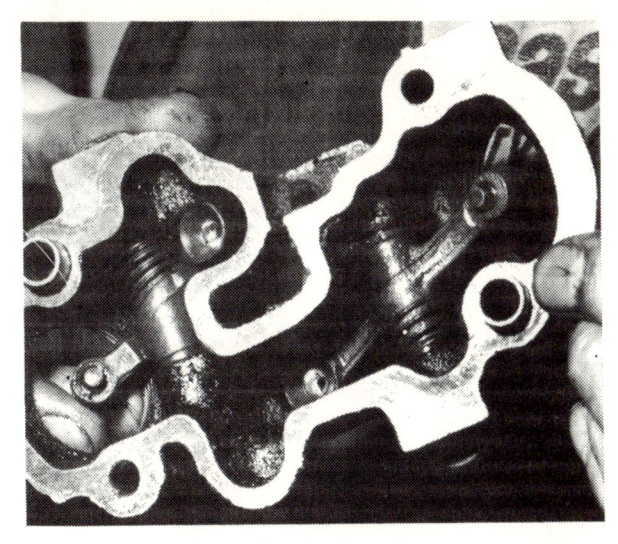

23.3. Examine ends of rockers for signs of wear

24.1. Dowel on camshaft ensures correct location with pinion

25 Timing pinions - examination

C200 and early CM90 models only:

1 It is unlikely that the timing pinions will need replacing unless the teeth have been damaged or broken.
2 Clean both pinions so that the timing marks are easily identified.

26 Gearbox components - examination

1 Give the gearbox components a close visual inspection for signs of wear or damage such as broken or chipped teeth, worn dogs, damaged or worn splines and bent selectors. Replace any parts found unserviceable since they cannot be reclaimed.
2 Examine the kickstarter return spring for weakness or damage. This component is often overlooked, even though it is tensioned every time the kickstarter is depressed.

27 Engine reassembly - general

1 Before reassembly is commenced, the various engine and gearbox components should be thoroughly clean and placed close to the working area.

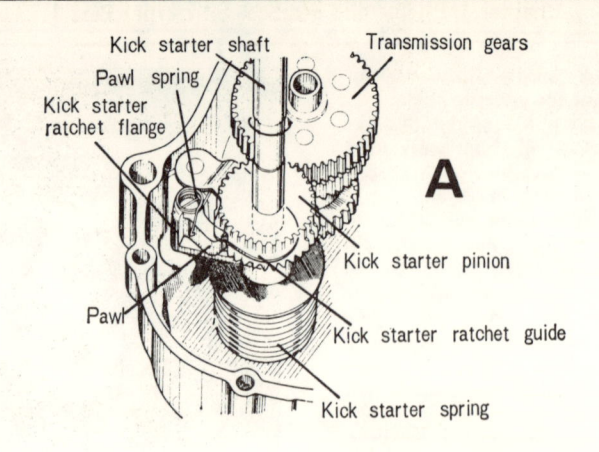

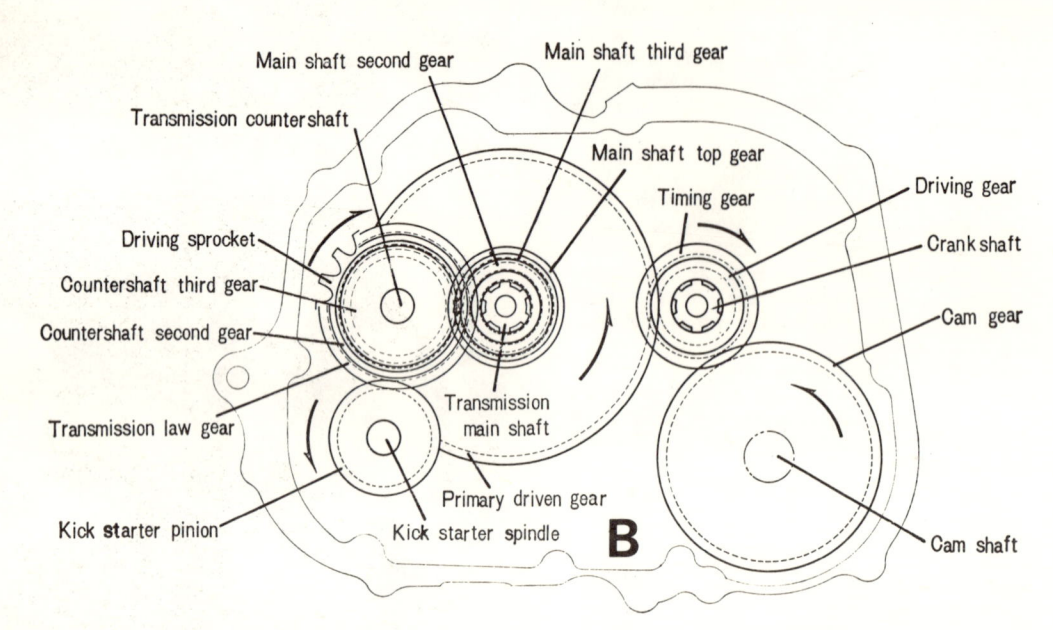

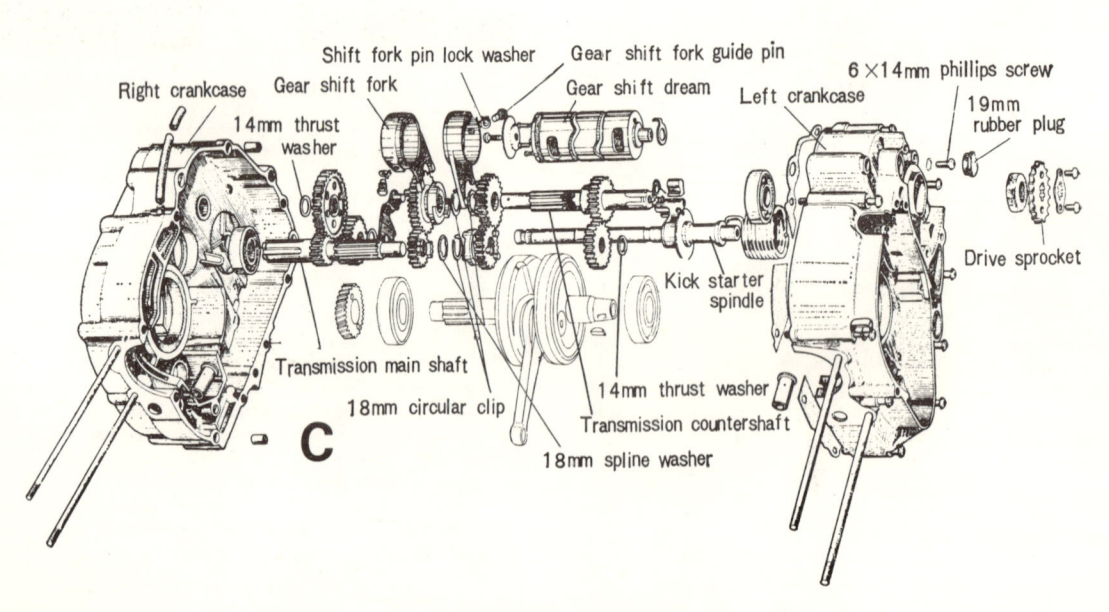

Fig. 1.3. A Kickstarter components
B Gear engagement
C Gearbox components

2 Make sure all traces of the old gaskets have been removed and the mating surfaces are clean and undamaged. One of the best ways to remove old gasket cement is to apply a rag soaked in methylated spirit. This acts as a solvent and will ensure the cement is removed without resort to scraping and the consequent risk of damage.
3 Gather together all the necessary tools and have available an oil can filled with clean engine oil. Make sure all the new gaskets and oil seals are to hand nothing is more frustrating than having to stop in the middle of a reassembly sequence because a vital gasket or replacement has been overlooked.
4 Make sure the reassembly area is clean and that there is adequate working space. Refer to the torque and clearance settings wherever they are given. Many of the smaller bolts are easily sheared if they are over-tightened. Always use the correct size screwdriver bit for the cross head screws and never an ordinary screwdriver or punch.

28.1. Use correct size drift when replacing bearings

28 Engine reassembly - fitting bearings to crankcases

1 Before fitting any of the crankcase bearings make sure that the bearing housings are scrupulously clean and that there are no burrs or lips on the entry to the housings. Press or drive the bearings into the cases using a mandrel and hammer, after first making sure that they are lined up squarely. Warming the crankcases will help when a bearing is a particularly tight fit.
2 When the bearings have been driven home, lightly oil them and make sure they revolve smoothly. This is particularly important in the case of the main bearings.
3 Using a soft mandrel, drive the oil seals into their respective housings. Do not use more force than is necessary because the seals damage very easily.
4 Lightly oil all the other moving parts as a prelude to reassembly. This will ensure all working parts are lubricated adequately during the initial start-up of the rebuilt engine.

29.3. Check screwed pins are tight and retained by tab washers

29 Engine reassembly - left-hand crankcase

1 Place the left-hand crankcase on two wooden blocks or in an engine stand so that the inner side faces upwards.
2 Assemble the gear clusters on their respective gear shafts, following the order detailed in Section 14 of this Chapter.
3 Locate the gear selector forks on the gear selector drum, making sure that the 10 mm screwed pins engage with the tracks in the selector drum. Tab washers retain these pins in position. The two selector forks are arranged on the selector drum in the back-to-back position.
4 Engage the selector forks in their respective positions, with the sliding dog on the layshaft and second gear on the mainshaft. Viewed endwise the lower of the two selector forks engages with the sliding dog on the layshaft and the upper fork with the sliding second gear pinion on the mainshaft.
5 Holding the complete gear assembly in the right hand, locate the layshaft in the journal ball bearing, the mainshaft in the plain bush and the tapered end of the selector drum in its housing. Hold all these parts firmly in position and invert the crankcase so that the 10 mm bolt and washer can be replaced in the centre of the selector drum. Tighten this bolt and fit the rubber blanking plug.
6 Re-invert the crankcase, so that the inside is again facing uppermost.

29.4. Engage selectors with gear cluster before assembly

30 Engine reassembly - fitting the kickstarter shaft assembly

1 If the ratchet assembly has been dismantled and the pawl carrier removed from the kickstarter shaft, it must be replaced so that the centre punch marks on the carrier and shaft coincide. Reassemble by reversing the sequel of events described in Section 13 of this Chapter. Position the complete assembly in the crankcase, making sure the dowel pin of the pawl lifting camplate engages with its housing in the crankcase.

31 Engine reassembly - fitting the crankshaft assembly

1 Fit the crankshaft assembly in the left-hand crankcase with the splined mainshaft uppermost. Make sure the connecting rod clears the aperture for the cylinder barrel spigot. It may be necessary to tap the assembly into position, if the crankshaft journal ball bearing is a tight fit in the steel outer ring.
2 Replace the exhaust valve cam follower in its housing. Give the stem a liberal coating of oil before insertion; this will help retain the follower in position whilst reassembly continues.
3 Replace the crankcase dowels and fit a new gasket, after checking that both mating faces of the crankcases are clean. It should not be necessary to use gasket cement.
4 Replace the inlet valve cam follower in the right-hand crankcase, oiling the stem to aid its retention.
5 Lower the right-hand crankcase on to the left-hand crankcase, without using force. It should locate readily if the instructions given have been followed carefully.
6 Replace the nine cross head screws that hold the two crankcases together and tighten down evenly. Make sure that the crankshaft assembly is still free to revolve and that the kickstarter spindle does not bind. If the latter is tight, it is probable that a thrust washer has been misplaced. The crankcases must be parted again to investigate and eliminate the cause.
7 Replace the gearbox final drive sprocket on the splined end of the layshaft. Fit the locating plate and the two 10 mm bolts.

32 Engine reassembly - fitting the piston and cylinder barrel

1 Assemble the piston on the connecting rod, with the arrow on the piston crown facing downwards. It may be necessary to heat the piston in warm water to enable the gudgeon pin to enter the piston bosses. Replace the gudgeon pin circlips, checking to ensure that both circlips are located positively in their grooves. Always fit new circlips - never re-use the originals. It is advisable to cover the mouth of the crankcase with rag during this operation. If a circlip falls in, it may be necessary to dismantle the engine again!
2 Check the piston ring gaps with the details given on their packing. Assemble the rings in their respective grooves, checking to make sure that the TOP marking on both compression rings faces upwards. The chrome ring is carried in the top groove of the piston and the tapered ring in the second groove. The slotted oil control ring occupies the bottom groove.
3 Fit a new cylinder base gasket and oil the piston and the cylinder bore. Slide the cylinder barrel down the long holding down studs and with the piston in a convenient position lower the barrel over the piston whilst compressing the piston rings with the fingers. Check that the ring gaps are staggered and not in line with each other, to cut down compression loss. Special care is needed whilst the rings are being compressed and inserted into the barrel because they are brittle and will break very easily.

33 Engine reassembly - replacing camshaft and camshaft pinion

C200 and early CM90 models:
1 Replace the camshaft pinion drive pin in the crankshaft and drive on the camshaft pinion so that it lines up with the pin. This task is made easier if the pinion is warmed before it is drifted into position.

30.1. Dowel pin must locate with housing

31.2. Replace exhaust valve cam follower after lubricating stem

31.4. Inlet cam follower must be fitted before right-hand crankcase is positioned

31.7. Oil seal can be fitted at this stage

31.7A. Locking plate retains gearbox sprocket on splined shaft

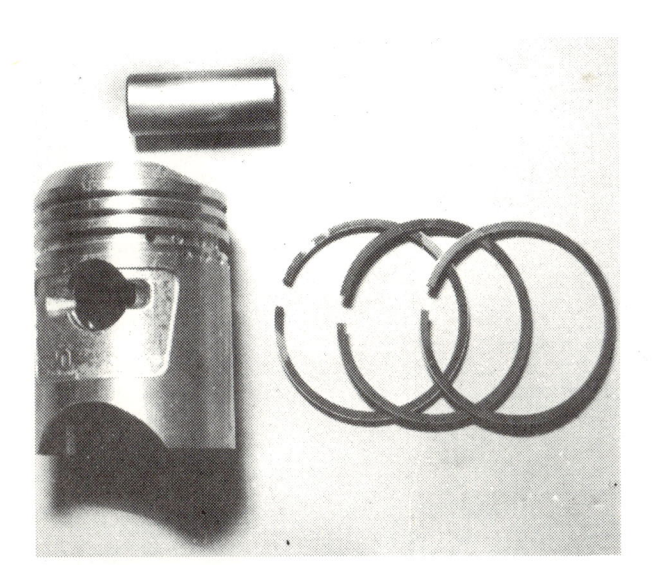

32.1. Piston assembly prior to fitting

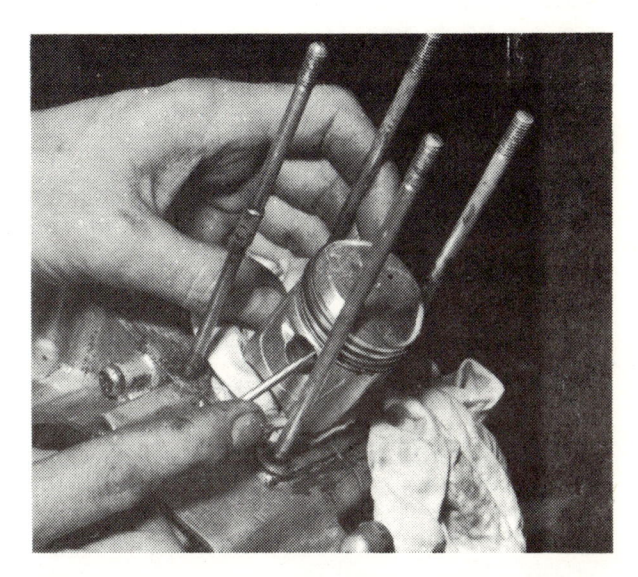

32.1A. Rag in crankcase mouth prevents misplaced circlip dropping in

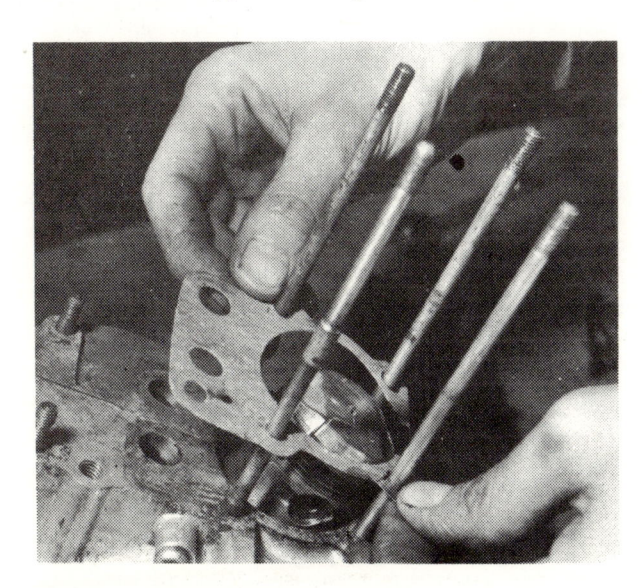

32.3. New cylinder base gasket is essential

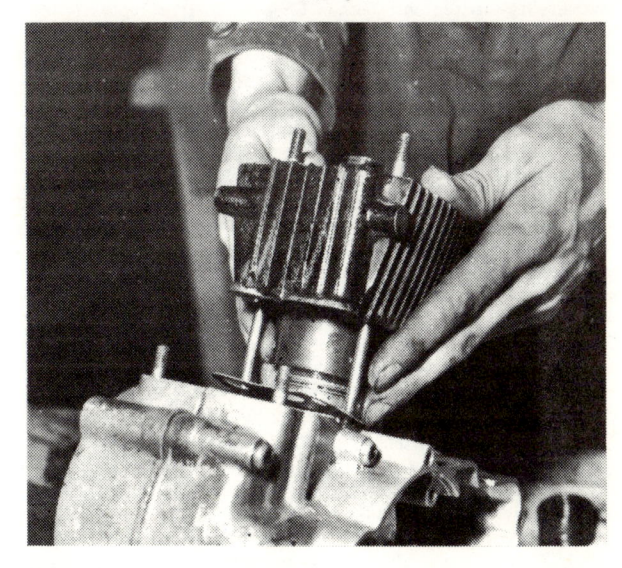

32.3A. Slide barrel down studs making sure rings are not trapped

2 Make sure the cam followers are home fully in their housings, then insert the camshaft so that the timing marks on the crankshaft pinion and the camwheel are exactly in line. This is important because the correct alignment of these marks determines the accuracy of the valve timing.
3 Early models have centre punch marks which register when the timing is correct. Later models employ an 'O' mark scribed on the camwheel which registers with either a similar 'O' mark on the crankshaft pinion, or, in the absence of any marking, with the threaded extractor hole nearest to the keyway in the pinion.
4 Replace the short oil pipe that lubricates these pinions and its retainer.

34 Engine reassembly - fitting gear change assembly

1 Check that the thrust washer is in position on the gear change shaft and tape the splined end of the shaft so that it will not damage the oil seal as it passes through. Whilst passing the shaft through the crankcase depress the gear change lever so that it will locate in the slot at the end of the selector drum.
2 Refit the selector drum pawl and spring, making sure the pawl engages with the gear indexing pin plate.

35 Engine reassembly - fitting and tensioning kickstarter return spring

1 Lower the kickstarter return spring over the kickstarter shaft, locating the inner tang of the spring in the milled slot of the shaft before pressing the spring home.
2 Tension the spring by twisting the end of the spring in an anti-clockwise direction, until the end can be looped in the abutment at the base of the casting. Fit the retaining washer and circlip.
3 At this stage it is important to check whether the gear change and kickstarter mechanisms function correctly and that the gearbox shafts, crankshaft etc still revolve freely.

36 Engine reassembly - locating the driver gear and clutch assembly

1 Lower the large driving gear on to the splined gearbox mainshaft and refit the retaining circlip. Make sure the circlip is a good fit; if in any doubt, fit a replacement.
2 If the clutch has been dismantled, reassemble by reversing the dismantling instructions given in Chapter 2. After replacing the bronze bush in the centre of the drive gear and the drive gear itself, position the complete clutch assembly on the mainshaft and replace the locking washer and sleeve nut. Tighten the nut and bend over one of the tabs of the lock washer.
3 Press the journal ball bearing carrier into the centre of the clutch drum and the bearing itself. C200 and early CM90 models, or:
Fit the clutch outer plate gasket and the outer plate itself. Press the journal ball bearing into the centre of the cover plate.
4 Position the clutch operating lever and washer on the splined gear lever pedal shaft and place the anti-rattle spring in the centre of the clutch operating cam plate. CM90, C90 and C70 models.
5 Replace the two dowel pins in the outer side of the crankcase and position the new clutch cover gasket. Lower the cover over the crankcase, taking care that the kickstarter oil seal in the cover is not damaged (lightly grease end of shaft). Tighten the nine cross head screws that retain the clutch cover in place.

37 Engine reassembly - fitting a.c. generator

C200, CM90, C90, S90 and C70 models:
1 Fit the woodruff key in the crankshaft and slide the generator rotor on to the crankshaft.

2 Place the automatic advance and retard unit on the top face of the rotor, so that the pin in the base of the mechanism registers with the hole in the face of the rotor. (C200 and early CM90 models only).
3 Replace the central 14 mm retaining bolts and washer and tighten, whilst holding the rotor firmly with a chain wrench or some similar tool. Check that the advance and retard mechanism operates smoothly and freely. (C200 and early CM90 models only).
4 Locate the stator coil assembly in the crankcase housing so that the timing pointer is to the rear of the engine. Replace and tighten the three cross head screws that hold the stator coil assembly in position. Locate the cable harness grommet in the crankcase slot made for this purpose and connect the green wire to the spring loaded end contact of the neutral indicator contact.

C200 and early CM90 models only:
5 Make sure the blue wire to the condenser is threaded through the inspection aperture. Tighten the four cross head screws that retain the cover to the crankcase.

C200 and early CM90 models only:
6 Position the contact breaker plate in the housing. Replace and tighten the two cross head retaining screws.

C70 and S65 models:
1 Position the stator plate and coil assembly in the outer crankcase, making sure that it is pressed home fully before the two countersunk retaining screws are tightened.
2 Fit the woodruff key in the crankshaft, locate the flywheel on the crankshaft, replace the retaining nut and washer and tighten fully whilst holding the flywheel firmly with a chain wrench or some similar tool.

38 Engine reassembly - setting the contact breaker points

Reference to Chapter 4, section 3 will show how the contact breaker points can be adjusted to a gap of 0.014 inch when they are fully open. This check, and if necessary, adjustment must always be made before the ignition timing can be set.

39 Engine reassembly - checking and resetting the ignition timing

This operation is described fully in Chapter 4, section 6. The need for accuracy cannot be over-stressed because even a relatively small error in setting will have a marked effect on the performance of any small capacity engine.

40 Engine reassembly - fitting the cylinder head and rocker box

C200 and early CM90 models:
1 Assuming the cylinder head has received the attention described in Sections 21 to 23 of this Chapter, it can be replaced on the cylinder barrel.
2 Place a new copper cylinder head gasket in the spigot joint, using a coating of oil to hold it in place during reassembly. Replace also the two 'O' rings at the top of the push rod tunnels and a further seal ring over the oil drainaway.
3 Slide the cylinder head down the long holding down studs, making sure that none of the seals or gaskets are displaced.
4 Replace the pushrods, making sure they register with the tunnels inside the cam followers. The shorter exhaust pushrod fits in the left-hand side.
5 Fit a new rocker box gasket and lower the rocker box on to the cylinder head, so that the ends of the pushrods engage with the cups in the ends of the rocker arms.
6 Replace the cylinder head and rocker box retaining nuts. Tighten them gradually in a diagonal sequence. Do not tighten beyond the recommended torque setting (6.5 to 8.7 lb ft) or the studs may shear.

33.3. Timing marks in register make timing easy

35.2. Loop spring over crankcase abutment to provide correct tension

35.2A. Do not omit thrust washer

35.2B. Circlip retains kickstarter spring assembly

35.3. Check gear change and kickstarter operations at this stage

36.1. Lower driving gear on gearbox mainshaft splines

36.2. Oil bronze bush before replacing drive gear

37.4. Locate stator coil assembly after replacing rotor

37.4A. Connect green wire to neutral indicator contact

37.5. Thread through blue wire and connect to condenser

40.1. Cylinder head ready for assembly

40.2. New copper head gasket is essential

40.2A. New seals for push rod tunnels

40.2B. New seal also for oil drainaway

40.3. Slide head down retaining studs

41.3. Use new 'O' ring seals for both rocker box caps

43. Make sure exhaust pipe joint has new sealing ring

41 Engine reassembly - adjusting the tappets

1   The tappets should be adjusted to 0.002 inch clearance when the engine is cold and the piston is at top dead centre (TDC) on the compression stroke.

2   To adjust the tappets, slacken the lock nut at the end of the rocker arm and turn the square-ended adjuster until the clearance is correct, as measured by a feeler gauge. Hold the

square-ended adjuster firmly when the lock nut is tightened, otherwise it will move and the adjustment will be lost.
3 After completing the adjustment to both valves, refit and tighten the rocker box caps, using new 'O' ring seals. Use a spanner that is a good fit otherwise the caps will damage easily.

42 Engine reassembly - completion and final adjustments

1 Refit the rocker oil feed pipe and tighten the two union bolts.
2 Replace the sparking plug after checking that it is gapped at 0.024 inch.
3 Replace and tighten the crankcase drain plug. Refill the sump with clean engine oil of the recommended viscosity. The capacity is 0.7 litres, just under one Imperial pint. Check with the dipstick to make sure the oil is at the correct level.

43 Refitting the engine/gearbox unit in the frame

Follow in reverse the procedure given in section 5 of this Chapter.

44 Starting and running the rebuilt engine

When the initial start-up is made, run the engine gently for the first few minutes in order to allow the oil to circulate throughout all parts of the engine. Remember that if a number of new parts have been fitted or if the engine has been rebored, it will be necessary to follow the original running-in instructions so that the new parts have ample opportunity to bed-down in a satisfactory manner. Check for oil leaks and/or blowing gaskets before the machine is run on the road.

Fault diagnosis for both engines and gearbox appears after Part 2 on page 46

Chapter 1 Engine and gearbox (ohc type) Part 2

Contents

General description ... 45	Camshaft chain tensioner - examination and renovation ... 68
Operations with engine in frame ... 46	Trochoid oil pump - removal and replacement ... 69
Operations with engine removed ... 47	Engine reassembly - general ... 70
Method of engine/gearbox removal ... 48	Fitting bearings to crankcases ... 71
Removing the engine/gearbox unit ... 49	Engine reassembly - left-hand crankcase ... 72
Dismantling the engine and gearbox - general .. 50	Engine reassembly - fitting the kickstarter shaft assembly ... 73
Engine and gearbox dismantling - removal of generator ... 51	Engine reassembly - fitting the crankshaft assembly ... 74
Cylinder head and cylinder - removal ... 52	Engine reassembly - fitting the piston and cylinder barrel ... 75
Piston and piston rings - removal ... 53	Engine reassembly - fitting the gear change assembly.. 76
Valves and rockers - removal ... 54	Engine reassembly - fitting and tensioning the kickstarter return spring ... 77
Crankcases - separating ... 55	
Crankshaft assembly - removal ... 56	Engine reassembly - locating the driver gear and clutch assembly ... 78
Kickstarter shaft and ratchet assembly - removal ... 57	
Gear selector drum and gear cluster - removal ... 58	Engine reassembly - fitting the cylinder head .. 79
Oil seals - removal ... 59	Engine reassembly - timing the overhead camshaft (valve timing) ... 80
Crankshaft and gearbox main bearings - removal ... 60	
Examination and renovation - general ... 61	Engine reassembly - adjusting the tappets ... 81
Big-end and main bearings - examination and renovation ... 62	Engine reassembly - fitting flywheel generator ... 82
Cylinder barrel - examination and renovation ... 63	Engine reassembly - checking and resetting the ignition timing ... 83
Piston and rings - examination and renovation ... 64	
Valves, valve seats and valve guides - examination and renovation ... 65	Engine reassembly - completion and final adjustments ... 84
	Starting and running the rebuilt engine ... 85
Cylinder head - decarbonisation and examination ... 66	Fault diagnosis - engines.. ... 86
Rockers and rocker shafts - examination ... 67	Fault diagnosis - gearbox.. ... 87

Specifications

Engine (ohc type)

Type ...	Single cylinder overhead camshaft, chain operated
Cylinder head ..	Aluminium alloy
Cylinder barrel ...	Cast iron
Bore ...	44 mm (S65)
	47 mm (C70)
	50 mm (C90, S90 and CM90)
Stroke ...	41.4 mm (S65 and C70)
	45.6 mm (C90, S90 and CM90)
Capacity ...	63 cc (S65)
	72 cc (C70)
	89.6 cc (C90, S90 and CM90)
Bhp ...	6.2 @ 10,000 rpm (S65)
	6.2 @ 9,000 rpm (C70)
	7.5 @ 9,500 rpm (CM90 and C90)
	8 @ 9,000 rpm (S90)
Compression ratio ...	8.1 : 1 (S65 and C70)
	8.2 : 1 (CM90, S90 and C90)

Crankshaft

Crankpin outside diameter ...	0.9099 - 0.9105 inch (23.098 - 23.112 mm)

Connecting rod

Big-end end float ...	0.004 - 0.014 inch (0.1 mm - 0.35 mm)
Small end and gudgeon pin clearance ...	0.001 - 0.002 inch (0.025 - 0.050 mm)
Small end bore diameter ...	0.5124 - 0.5135 inch (13.016 - 13.043 mm) (65 cc and 70 cc models)
	0.5517 - 0.5523 inch (14.012 - 14.028 mm) (90 cc models)

Piston

Diameter of crown ...	1.708 - 1.710 inch (43.0 - 43.5 mm) (S65 model)
Maximum diameter at base of skirt ...	1.733 - 1.734 inch (43.980 - 44.0 mm) (S65 model)
	1.9673 - 1.9681 inch (49.97 - 49.99 mm) (90 cc models)

Piston to cylinder clearance (minimum)	0.0004 inch (0.01 mm) Replace if over 0.004 inch (0.1 mm)
Oversize pistons available	+0.25 mm, +0.50 mm, +0.75 mm and +1.00 mm
Piston and gudgeon pin clearance	0.00008 - 0.00055 inch (0.002 - 0.014 mm)

Piston rings

Compression (two top rings)	Top ring chrome, second ring tapered
Oil control ring	Third ring, at top of skirt

Gudgeon pin

Diameter	0.5121 - 0.5123 inch (13.002 - 13.008 mm)

Valves

Tappet clearance, inlet and exhaust	0.002 inch, set with engine cold
Seat angle	45°
Inlet, overall length	2.540 inch (64.5 mm) (S65 model) 2.648 inch (67.3 mm) (90 cc models)
Outside diameter of stem	0.217 inch (5.5 mm) (S65 models) 0.215 inch (5.45 mm) (90 cc models)
Exhaust, overall length	2.483 inch (63.9 mm) (S65 model) 2.597 inch (67.3 mm) (90 cc models)
Outside diameter of stem	0.217 inch (5.5 mm) (S65 models) 0.214 inch (5.43 mm) (90 cc models)
Stem and guide clearance (inlet)	0.0004 - 0.0012 inch (0.010 - 0.030 mm)
Stem and guide clearance (exhaust)	0.0012 - 0.0020 inch (0.030 - 0.050 mm)
Spring (outer) free length	1.110 inch (28.1 mm) (S65 model) 1.253 inch (31.8 mm) (90 cc models)
Spring (inner) free length	1.01 inch (25.5 mm) (S65 model) 1.044 inch (26.5 mm) (90 cc models)

Capacities

Engine and gearbox (in unit)	0.9 litres (1.58 Imp. pints) (1.90 U.S. pints)

Torque wrench settings

Cylinder head nuts	6.5 - 8.7 ft lb
Cylinder head left side cover	5.8 - 8.7 ft lb
Cylinder head right hand side cover	5.1 - 6.5 ft lb
Carburettor mounting studs	60 in lb

This section relates specifically to the overhead camshaft engine. It replaced the pushrod ohv engine, as described earlier.

Although there are quite fundamental design differences between the two types of engine there are many similarities with regard to the procedure for dismantling, examination, renovation and reassembly. These have been covered fully in the first part of this Chapter, with subdivisions according to model, where appropriate. Detailed below are the items that relate exclusively to the overhead camshaft engine; the gearbox unit can be regarded as identical, regardless of the type of engine used.

45 General description

The Honda CM90 (late models) C90, S90, C70 and S65 models are fitted with an overhead camshaft engine in which the valve mechanism is chain driven. The camshaft is located within the aluminium alloy cylinder head; with this arrangement it is necessary to disturb the valve timing when the cylinder head is removed. A gear or a trochoid oil pump is included in the general specification of the engine, to provide a pressure oil feed in addition to lubrication by splash. There is also two filters in the lubrication system, a gauze screen in the crankcase and a centrifugal filter within the clutch centre.

46 Operations with engine in frame

Refer to section 2.

47 Operations with engine removed

Refer to section 3.

48 Method of engine/gearbox removal

Refer to section 4.

49 Removing the engine/gearbox unit

Refer to section 5.

50 Dismantling the engine and gearbox - general

Refer to section 6.

45. Camshaft is located within cylinder head casting

45A. Oil pump is fitted behind clutch

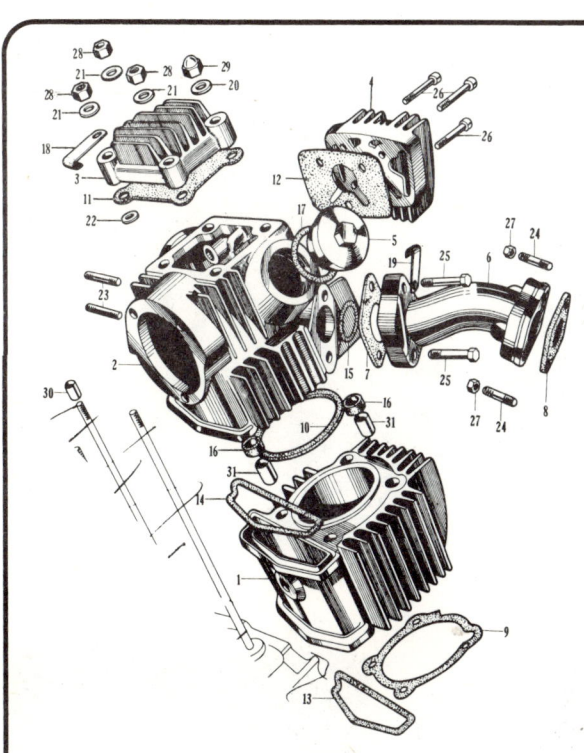

Fig. 1.4. Cylinder and cylinder head

1 Cylinder barrel
2 Cylinder head
3 Cylinder head top cover
4 Right-hand side cover
5 Rocker box cap
6 Induction pipe
7 Carburettor gasket
8 Carburettor heat insulator
9 Cylinder base gasket
10 Cylinder head gasket
11 Cylinder head top cover gasket
12 Right-hand side cover gasket
13 Bottom cam chain chamber gasket
14 Top cam chain chamber gasket
15 'O' ring for induction pipe
16 Cylinder stud gasket
17 'O' ring for rocker box cap
18 Clip for carburettor overflow tube
19 Clip for sparking plug lead
20 Sealing washer for cylinder head nuts
21 Flat washer for cylinder head nuts
22 'O' ring for cylinder head studs
23 Exhaust pipe studs
24 Induction pipe studs
25 Bolts for induction pipe
26 Side cover bolts
27 Nuts for induction pipe studs
28 Cylinder head nuts
29 Dome nut for cylinder head
30 Dowel pin for cylinder studs
31 Dowel pin for cylinder head

Note: The 65 cc and 70 cc engines differ in a number of minor respects, mainly with regard to the location of the contact breaker assembly and the design of the side covers

Fig. 1.5. Crankshaft, connecting rod and piston

1 Crankpin
2 Left-hand crankshaft
3 Right-hand crankshaft
4 Blanking plug for crankpin
5 Connecting rod
6 Big-end bearing cage
7 Piston
8 Gudgeon pin
9 Circlips
10 Piston rings
11 Lower camshaft chain sprocket
12 Oil seal
13 Woodruff key
14 Big-end rollers
15 Main bearings

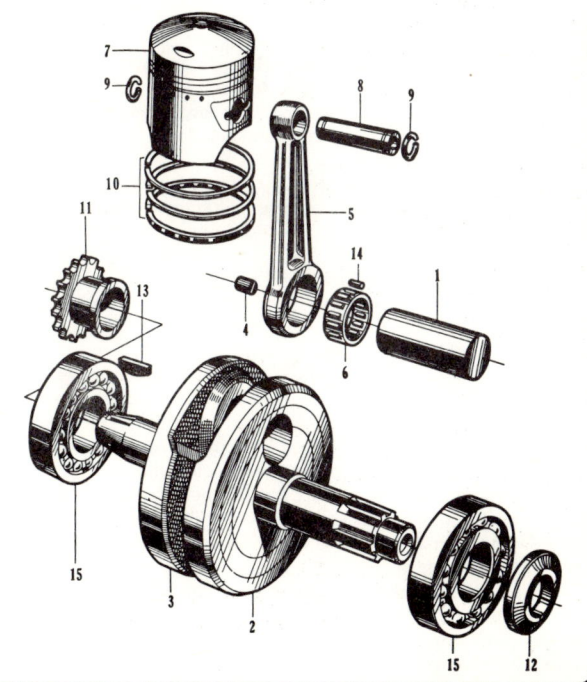

51 Engine and gearbox dismantling - removal of generator

Refer to section 7.

52 Cylinder head and cylinder - removal

C70 and S65 models only:

1 Before the cylinder head can be detached, it is necessary to remove the overhead camshaft drive, top sprocket, complete with timing chain. Commence dismantling by removing the flywheel generator as described in section 7.
2 Remove the 6 mm bolt from the centre of the right-hand (finned) camshaft cover. This passes right through the camshaft and when withdrawn will permit the left-hand (circular) cover to be removed.
3 Remove also the right-hand (finned) cover, after unscrewing the two cross head screws.
4 Rotate the crankshaft so that the piston is at top dead centre and check whether the 'O' mark at the edge of the top camshaft sprocket is in line with the centre of the camshaft and the centre of the crankshaft. It may be necessary to rotate the engine several times until the 'O' mark exactly coincides with this centre line when the piston is at top dead centre (TDC).
5 Unscrew the three 6 mm bolts that retain the camshaft drive top sprocket to the camshaft and withdraw the camshaft, leaving the sprocket and chain in the cylinder head.
6 Remove the cylinder head nuts and the bolt on the left hand side at the cylinder head/barrel joint. Withdraw the cylinder head, allowing the camshaft sprocket and chain to drop through their tunnel in the casting.
7 Never loosen the cylinder head before the camshaft is removed.
8 Remove the 6 mm bolt and washer from the left-hand side of the cylinder barrel, and draw out the cam chain guide roller. The cylinder barrel can now be slid along the holding down studs until it is clear of the crankcase, after the bolt on the left-hand side of the base is withdrawn.

CM90, S90, C90 models only:

The contact breaker assembly of these models is located within the cylinder head casting, where it is driven from an extension of the overhead camshaft. In consequence, a special dismantling procedure is necessary, as follows.

1 Remove the circular contact breaker cover on the cylinder head, held by two cross-head screws. Remove also the left-hand crankcase cover, making allowance for any oil that may be released. The generator stator and rotor assemblies can now be withdrawn by following the procedure detailed in section 7, paragraphs 9 to 13.
2 Disconnect the lead wire to the contact breaker assembly and remove the contact breaker assembly complete with back plate. It is retained in position by two cross head screws, which should be removed.
3 Remove the automatic advance unit by withdrawing the hexagon head bolt from the centre of the camshaft. Remove also the dowel pin, which is used to ensure the assembly is replaced in the correct position.
4 Detach the contact breaker outer casting and gasket, which is held to the cylinder head casting by three cross head screws. Rotate the crankshaft so that the woodruff key slot is exactly in line with the dowel pin hole and the centre of the camshaft.
5 Remove the camshaft pinion by unscrewing the two 6 mm bolts that retain it to the camshaft flange. The driving chain can be left in position; the sprocket and chain will fall clear of the cylinder head when the latter is lifted, after they have cleared the end of the camshaft.
6 Continue by following the procedure outlined for the S65 model, commencing with paragraph 7. Note that the dismantling of the camshaft assembly must be carried out with the cylinder head nuts fully tightened.

52.5. Remove camshaft sprocket before slackening cylinder head nuts

52.6. Keep sprocket with chain when removing cylinder head

52.8. Pin releases cam chain guide roller

Fig. 1.6. Camshaft and valves

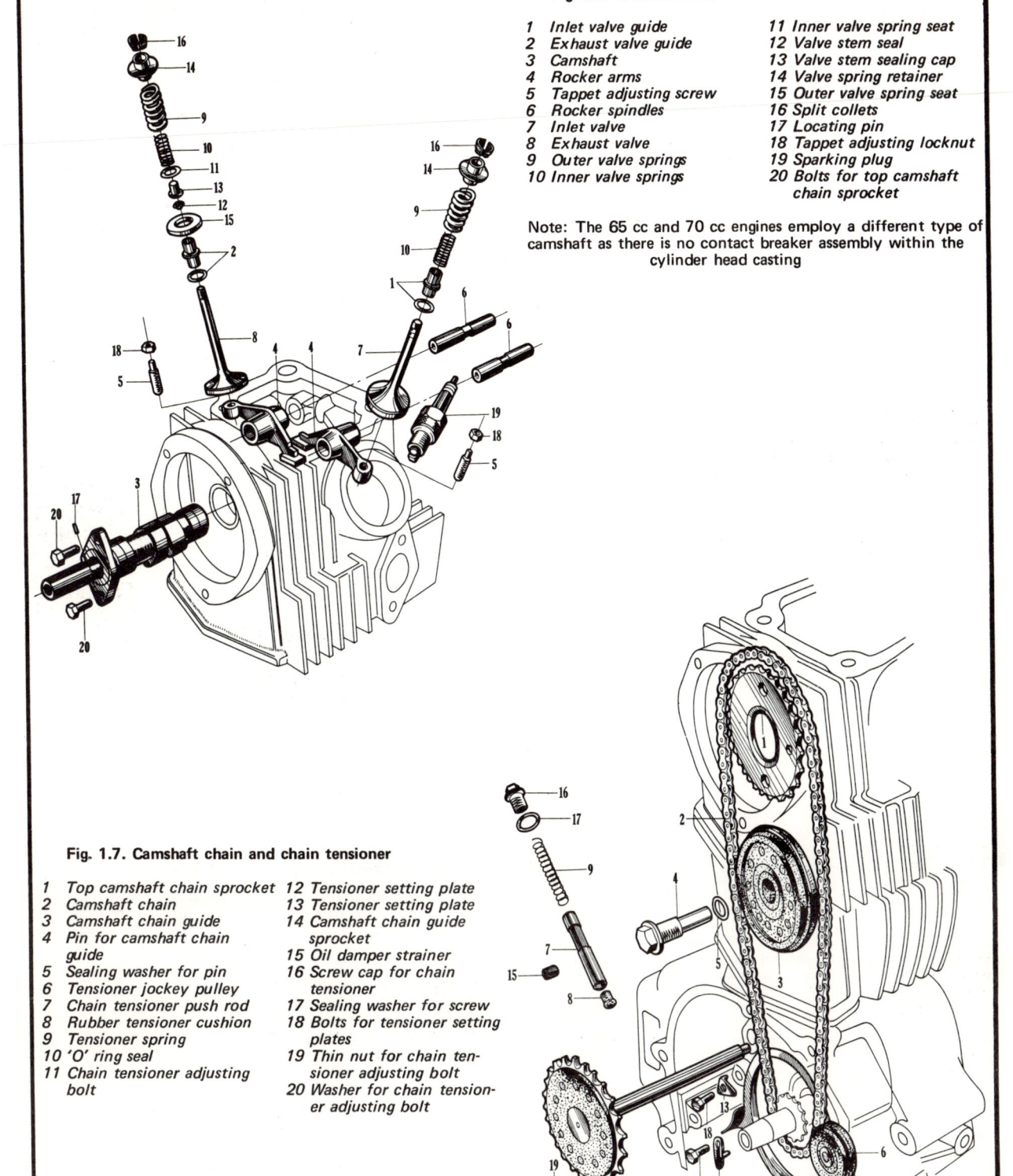

1. Inlet valve guide
2. Exhaust valve guide
3. Camshaft
4. Rocker arms
5. Tappet adjusting screw
6. Rocker spindles
7. Inlet valve
8. Exhaust valve
9. Outer valve springs
10. Inner valve springs
11. Inner valve spring seat
12. Valve stem seal
13. Valve stem sealing cap
14. Valve spring retainer
15. Outer valve spring seat
16. Split collets
17. Locating pin
18. Tappet adjusting locknut
19. Sparking plug
20. Bolts for top camshaft chain sprocket

Note: The 65 cc and 70 cc engines employ a different type of camshaft as there is no contact breaker assembly within the cylinder head casting

Fig. 1.7. Camshaft chain and chain tensioner

1. Top camshaft chain sprocket
2. Camshaft chain
3. Camshaft chain guide
4. Pin for camshaft chain guide
5. Sealing washer for pin
6. Tensioner jockey pulley
7. Chain tensioner push rod
8. Rubber tensioner cushion
9. Tensioner spring
10. 'O' ring seal
11. Chain tensioner adjusting bolt
12. Tensioner setting plate
13. Tensioner setting plate
14. Camshaft chain guide sprocket
15. Oil damper strainer
16. Screw cap for chain tensioner
17. Sealing washer for screw
18. Bolts for tensioner setting plates
19. Thin nut for chain tensioner adjusting bolt
20. Washer for chain tensioner adjusting bolt

53 Piston and piston rings - removal

Refer to section 9.

54 Valves and rockers - removal

1 The rocker arms are removed by withdrawing the rocker arm shafts, exposed when the right-hand (finned) camshaft cover is removed. They will push out of position.
2 The rocker arm bears direct on the cams, eliminating the need for any intermediary components.

55 Crankcases - separating

Refer to section 11. There is no need to remove either the oil pump located behind the clutch or the camshaft chain tensioner assembly found at the rear of the flywheel generator. Neither impede the separation of the crankcases.

56 Crankshaft assembly - removal

The crankshaft will have the bottom camshaft chain sprocket attached, in front of the left-hand main bearing.

57 Kickstarter shaft and ratchet assembly - removal

Refer to section 13.

58 Gear selector drum and gear cluster - removal

Refer to section 14.

59 Oil seals - removal

Refer to section 15.

60 Crankshaft and gearbox main bearings - removal

Refer to section 16.

61 Examination and renovation - general

Refer to section 17.

62 Big-end and main bearings - examination and renovation

Refer to section 18.

63 Cylinder barrel - examination and renovation

Refer to section 19.

64 Piston and rings - examination and renovation

Refer to section 20. Note that the overhead camshaft engine has different bore and stroke measurements from those of the pushrod ohv engine.

54.1. Removal of rocker spindles frees rocker arms

56. Crankshaft has bottom camshaft chain sprocket attached

65 Valves, valve seats and valve guides - examination and renovation

Refer to section 21.

66 Cylinder head - decarbonisation and examination

Refer to section 22. The camshaft will push out of the cylinder head casting if the cams are aligned with the special cutaways.

67 Rockers and rocker shafts - examination

Refer to section 23. The rockers fitted to the overhead camshaft engine are liable to show signs of greater wear at the camshaft end because there is no intermediary between the rocker arm and the face of the cam. Scuffing is the form of wear most likely to occur, unless the case hardened surface has broken through.

Fig. 1.8. Crankcases

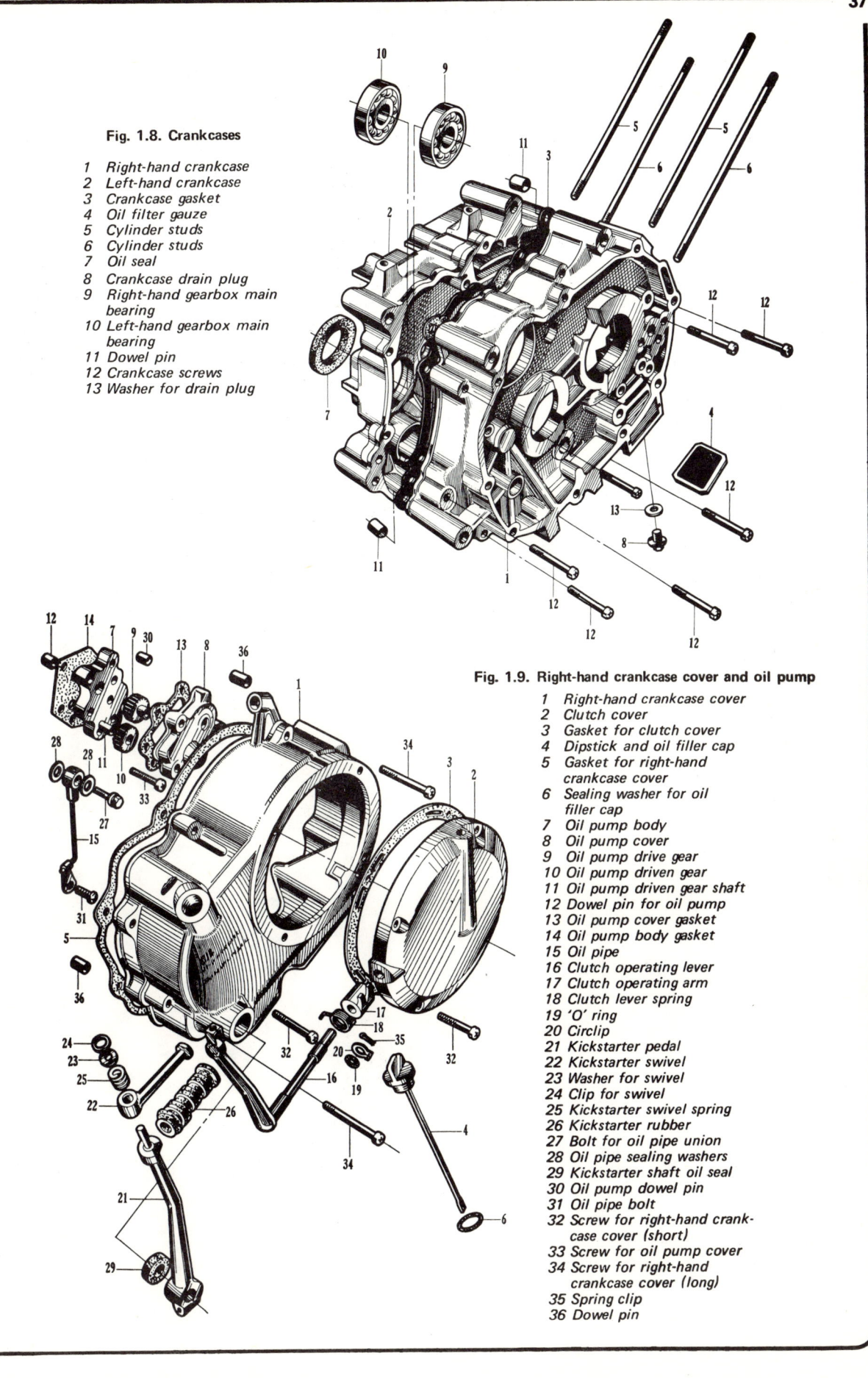

1 Right-hand crankcase
2 Left-hand crankcase
3 Crankcase gasket
4 Oil filter gauze
5 Cylinder studs
6 Cylinder studs
7 Oil seal
8 Crankcase drain plug
9 Right-hand gearbox main bearing
10 Left-hand gearbox main bearing
11 Dowel pin
12 Crankcase screws
13 Washer for drain plug

Fig. 1.9. Right-hand crankcase cover and oil pump

1 Right-hand crankcase cover
2 Clutch cover
3 Gasket for clutch cover
4 Dipstick and oil filler cap
5 Gasket for right-hand crankcase cover
6 Sealing washer for oil filler cap
7 Oil pump body
8 Oil pump cover
9 Oil pump drive gear
10 Oil pump driven gear
11 Oil pump driven gear shaft
12 Dowel pin for oil pump
13 Oil pump cover gasket
14 Oil pump body gasket
15 Oil pipe
16 Clutch operating lever
17 Clutch operating arm
18 Clutch lever spring
19 'O' ring
20 Circlip
21 Kickstarter pedal
22 Kickstarter swivel
23 Washer for swivel
24 Clip for swivel
25 Kickstarter swivel spring
26 Kickstarter rubber
27 Bolt for oil pipe union
28 Oil pipe sealing washers
29 Kickstarter shaft oil seal
30 Oil pump dowel pin
31 Oil pipe bolt
32 Screw for right-hand crankcase cover (short)
33 Screw for oil pump cover
34 Screw for right-hand crankcase cover (long)
35 Spring clip
36 Dowel pin

37

68 Camshaft chain tensioner - examination and renovation

1 An oil damped camshaft chain tensioner is employed, to fulfill the duel function of controlling the chain tension at high engine speeds and eliminating mechanical noise. A compression spring and pushrod within a guide provides the tension by bearing on one end of a pivoting arm which carries a jockey pulley on the other. The jockey pulley engages with the top run of the chain. The guide containing the spring and pushrod floods with oil when the engine is running, to provide the necessary damping medium.

2 The chain tensioner spring should have a free length of 3.04 inch. It should be replaced if the free length is reduced below 2.89 inches. To gain access to the spring and pushrod assembly, remove the 14 mm bolt that screws at an angle, into the base of the left hand crankcase.

3 Adjustment of the tensioner is automatic. Check that the tensioner is operating correctly when the left-hand flywheel generator cover and flywheel generator are removed.

4 The camshaft chain is of the endless variety and should not contain a split link.

69 Trochoid oil pump - removal and replacement

1 The trochoid oil pump is located behind the clutch, where it is retained to the right hand crankcase by three bolts. It is extremely unlikely that the pump will require attention and under normal circumstances it need not be removed during dismantling.

2 The pump comprises an inner and an outer rotor. The pumping action is provided by the differences in the shape and number of teeth between the inner and the outer rotors.

3 Early models employed a gear-type pump of similar outline, located in the same position.

4 There is a filter screen located horizontally in the bottom of the right-hand crankcase. This should be removed and cleaned.

70 Engine reassembly - general

Refer to section 27.

71 Fitting bearings to crankcases

Refer to section 28.

72 Engine reassembly - left-hand crankcase

Refer to section 29. A good check on the correct location of the mainshaft and layshaft thrust washers is provided by observing the mesh of the pinions on the uppermost ends of both shafts. If the thrust washers are in their correct positions, the pinions will be exactly in line with one another, and engage over the full width of their teeth.

73 Engine reassembly - fitting the kickstarter shaft assembly

Refer to section 30. The kickstarter shaft ratchet assembly differs in design, but is located in a similar manner to the dowel pin arrangement used for the push rod engines.

74 Engine reassembly - fitting the crankshaft assembly

Refer to section 31. The overhead camshaft engine does not require cam followers - paragraphs 2 and 4 can be omitted. Note also that the gearbox final drive sprocket is secured by a centre bolt that screws into the tapped layshaft. The locating plate is rivetted to the sprocket face.

72. Pinions will line up if thrust washers are located correctly

73. Kickstarter shaft design may differ on later models

74. Final drive sprocket is retained by centre bolt

75 Engine reassembly - fitting the piston and cylinder barrel

1   Refer to section 32. Before the piston is inserted into the cylinder barrel, the camshaft drive chain must be fitted to the crankshaft sprocket and fed through the tunnel cast in the cylinder barrel. The chain guide roller should also be fitted at this stage and located by the pin and 'O' ring seal that screws into the left-hand side of the cylinder barrel.
2   When the cylinder barrel is in position, the camshaft chain tensioning assembly can be fitted. Attach the chain tensioner arm and 'jockey' sprocket which is held in position by a screwed pivot bolt that engages with a tapped hole in the crankcase. Fit the tensioner push rod, tensioner spring and 14 mm bolt complete with new sealing washer. The tunnel is at an angle in the left-hand crankcase.

76 Engine reassembly - fitting the gear change assembly

1   Because the overhead camshaft engine is of different design from the push rod version, section 33 is no longer relevant and can be omitted completely. Continue reassembly by referring to section 34.
2   Note that a design change makes it necessary to fit the cam plate and pins to the gear selector drum after the crankcases have been joined together. The four pins are of equal length, but one will protrude further from the selector drum to act as a locating dowel. This arrangement ensures the cam plate on the end of the drum is in correct registration. The pawl roller and spring are attached after the end plate assembly is in position.

77 Engine reassembly - fitting and tensioning the kickstarter return spring

Refer to section 35. Design changes necessitate revised instructions. Slide the ratchet assembly over the splined section of the kickstarter shaft in any position and turn the shaft clockwise until the end of the spring retainer abuts on the stop that forms part of the crankcase casting. Loop the end of the return spring around the abutment above the kickstarter shaft assembly, whilst holding the shaft in the fully clockwise position. Fit the retaining circlip and check that both the kickstarter and the gear change mechanisms function correctly. In the case of the latter it will be necessary to revolve the gear shafts to facilitate correct engagement.

78 Engine reassembly - locating the driver gear and clutch assembly

1   Refer to section 36. Before the journal ball bearing carrier can be fitted, the clutch outer cover plate must be fitted, complete with a new gasket. This forms the seal to the centrifugal oil filter that is an integral part of the clutch centre. Do not omit the double diameter spacer behind the clutch.
2   It is assumed the oil pump has not been removed from the crankcase. If it has, the oil pump must be replaced before the clutch is lowered into position. Note there is a small oil pipe and locating plate on some models that directs oil to the primary transmission pinions. Do not omit the small but essential 'O' ring seal that is located over the spigot of the oil pipe union, at the point where it enters the pump.
3   There is no guide plate or retaining springs fitted to the overhead camshaft pinion.
4   Before the clutch outer cover is lowered into position, check that the oil filter screen has been slid into its holder within the crankcase.

75.1. Feed camshaft chain through tunnel in cylinder barrel

75.2. Jockey sprocket keeps cam chain tension constant

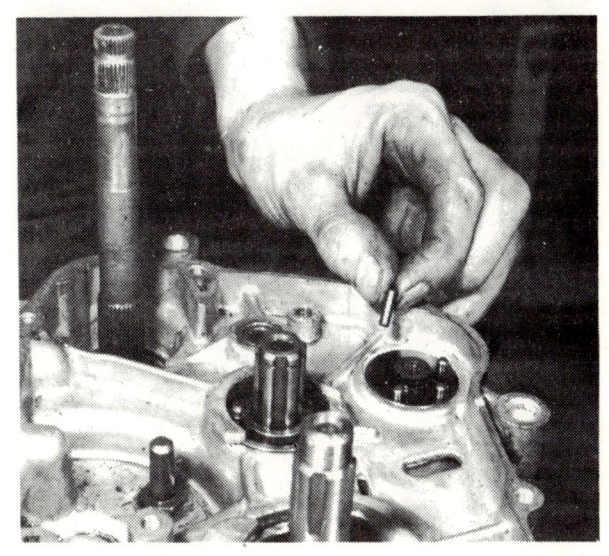

76.2. Fit pins first.......

76.2A. then plate, which registers with protruding pin.......

76.2B. Next add cam plate and retain with centre screw

76.2C. Pawl roller locates with cam plate cutaways

77. With spring retainer against stop, tension spring.......

77A. and loop around crankcase abutment

77B. Circlip holds complete assembly in position

78.1. Clutch outer cover forms seal to centrifugal oil filter

78.1A. Double diameter spacer fits behind clutch

78.2. Locating plate holds oil pipe in position

78.4. Oil filter screen slots into crankcase housing

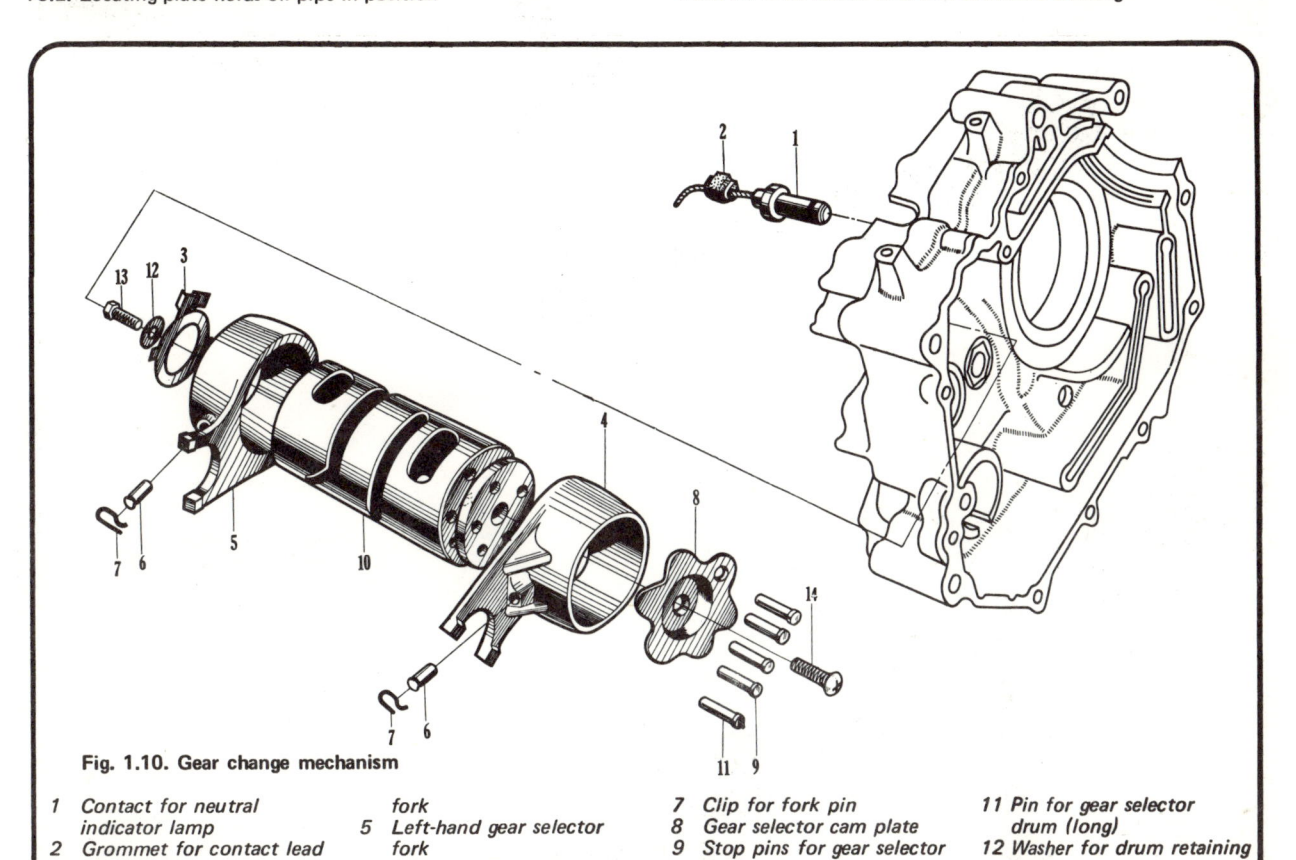

Fig. 1.10. Gear change mechanism

1. Contact for neutral indicator lamp
2. Grommet for contact lead
3. Neutral contact rotor
4. Right-hand gear selector fork
5. Left-hand gear selector fork
6. Pin for gear selector fork
7. Clip for fork pin
8. Gear selector cam plate
9. Stop pins for gear selector drum
10. Gear selector drum
11. Pin for gear selector drum (long)
12. Washer for drum retaining bolt
13. Drum retaining bolt
14. Screw for cam plate

Note: Minor differences may occur in the design of the gearbox components, depending on the model concerned

Fig. 1.11. Gear change mechanism

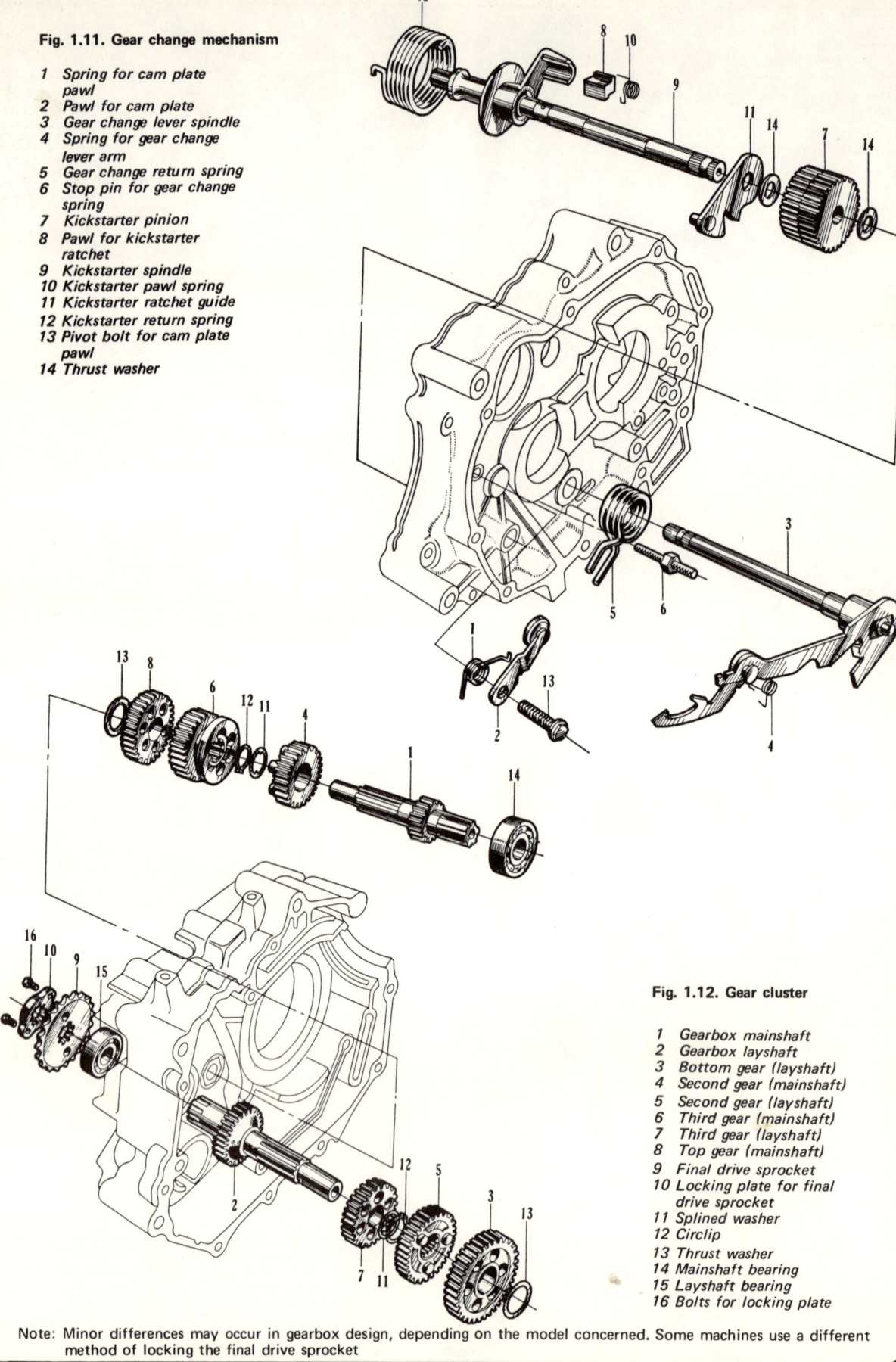

1. Spring for cam plate pawl
2. Pawl for cam plate
3. Gear change lever spindle
4. Spring for gear change lever arm
5. Gear change return spring
6. Stop pin for gear change spring
7. Kickstarter pinion
8. Pawl for kickstarter ratchet
9. Kickstarter spindle
10. Kickstarter pawl spring
11. Kickstarter ratchet guide
12. Kickstarter return spring
13. Pivot bolt for cam plate pawl
14. Thrust washer

Fig. 1.12. Gear cluster

1. Gearbox mainshaft
2. Gearbox layshaft
3. Bottom gear (layshaft)
4. Second gear (mainshaft)
5. Second gear (layshaft)
6. Third gear (mainshaft)
7. Third gear (layshaft)
8. Top gear (mainshaft)
9. Final drive sprocket
10. Locking plate for final drive sprocket
11. Splined washer
12. Circlip
13. Thrust washer
14. Mainshaft bearing
15. Layshaft bearing
16. Bolts for locking plate

Note: Minor differences may occur in gearbox design, depending on the model concerned. Some machines use a different method of locking the final drive sprocket

79 Engine reassembly - fitting the cylinder head

1 Before the cylinder head can be fitted to the engine it must be fully assembled. Although it may appear possible to replace the rockers when the cylinder head is bolted down, this is not so in practice. The rocker spindles are retained by the long holding down studs that pass through the cylinder head and cannot be removed or replaced unless the cylinder head is lifted.
2 Lower the cylinder head on to the cylinder barrel, taking care to feed the camshaft drive chain through the tunnel cast in the bottom of the head. It is necessary to loop the chain around the large camshaft sprocket during this operation, passing both through the tunnel. They can be kept together by passing a wire through the centre of the sprocket so that they are retained in close proximity to the camshaft, whilst the head is bolted down. The camshaft is fitted from the right-hand side of the cylinder head, where there is sufficient clearance for the cams to pass through.
3 Note that there is a full gasket between the cylinder barrel and head and not just a copper ring seal.
4 Fit the finned top cover of the cylinder head with gasket, and pull down evenly until the recommended torque settings are achieved (6.5 - 8.7 ft lb). Always tighten in a diagonal sequence, an essential requirement because an alloy cylinder head will distort easily. There is a separate bolt on the left-hand side of the cylinder head, just below the circular camshaft sprocket aperture, and below this, a bolt at the base of the cylinder barrel. Both must be tightened.

80 Engine reassembly - timing the overhead camshaft (valve timing)

1 Rotate the crankshaft until the keyway for the flywheel generator is exactly in line with a line drawn through the centre of the engine. This imaginary line passes through the centre of the camshaft and the centre of the crankshaft

2 Arrange the camshaft sprocket and chain on the camshaft so that the small 'O' stamped close to one of the sprocket teeth is in the twelve o'clock position with regard to the top of the cylinder head. The centre line mentioned in the paragraph above should pass also through the 'O' timing mark.
3 Without turning either the crankshaft or the camshaft pinion, rotate the camshaft itself until the three tapped holes in the left-hand flange (two holes, all models except C70 and S65) correspond exactly with the holes in the camshaft sprocket. Fit the bolts that clamp the sprocket to the camshaft and check again that all the timing positions correspond exactly with the centre line.
4 The need for extreme accuracy cannot be overstressed. Even a small error in this setting will have a very marked effect on the valve timing and therefore on the performance and general running of the engine.
5 If the second check proves satisfactory, the inner contact breaker housing can be fitted with its sealing gasket, (all models except C70 and S65). It is retained by three cross head screws. Note that an oil seal is fitted to the centre of the housing, to prevent oil from reaching the contact breaker assembly.
6 Slide the automatic advance mechanism over the camshaft, making sure it locates with the pin in the camshaft (all models except C70 and S65). Fit also the contact breaker plate and contact breaker assembly, then fit and tighten the centre bolt (complete with washer) that clamps the automatic advance unit to the camshaft.
7 Attach the lead wire to the contact breaker assembly, complete with rubber sealing grommet. It should pass through a clamp attached to the top left-hand cylinder head nut or some other convenient location (all models except C70 and S65). The right-hand finned cover plate can then be attached, using a new gasket. This cover is held by three cross head screws.
8 A somewhat different arrangement is adopted for the reassembly of the C70 and S65 engine; because the contact breaker and automatic advance unit is contained within the flywheel magneto generator. After following the above-mentioned timing procedure and clamping the sprocket to the camshaft with the three securing bolts, the two side covers can be fitted to the cylinder head, each with a new gasket. The right-hand cover is held by two cross head screws and can be fitted first. A long bolt passes through the centre of this cover and through the hollow centre of the camshaft. It locates with a tapped hole in the circular left-hand cover and is the sole means of clamping this latter cover in position.

81 Engine reassembly - adjusting the tappets

Refer to section 41.

82 Engine reassembly - fitting flywheel generator

1 Position the stator plate and coil assembly in the outer crankcase, retaining it in position with the countersunk screws. Fit the woodruff key in the crankshaft and locate the rotor. Replace the retaining nut and washer and tighten fully whilst holding the rotor firmly.
2 The flywheel magneto generator fitted to the C70 and S65 models is of different design. Before the rotor is located on the crankshaft, the action of the automatic advance unit should be checked. It is found within the rotor, where it forms an integral unit with the contact breaker cam.
3 Irrespective of the type of flywheel generator fitted, check that the piston is exactly at top dead centre when the 'T' mark on the flywheel rim or face corresponds with the line on the projection within the outer crankcase.

83 Engine reassembly - checking and resetting the ignition timing

1 Realign the flywheel rotor so that the 'F' mark inscribed on the flywheel rim or face exactly corresponds with the line on the projection within the outer crankcase. If the engine is on the compression stroke (both valves closed) the contact breaker points should be separating. Refer to Chapter 4, sections 4 and 7, if adjustment is required. When the correct setting has been achieved and re-checked, the left-hand cylinder head cover plate can be replaced, using a new gasket. This plate is retained by two cross head screws (all models except C70 and S65).
2 Refit the crankcase outer cover, using a new gasket. Refit also the generator inspection cover if it too has been removed. Again a new gasket is required. The cover fitted to the C70 and S65 models does not have a separate generator inspection cover, nor does it contain the oil seal for the spindle of the gear change pedal.
3 The engine is now ready for replacement in the frame by reversing the procedure given in section 5 of this Chapter.

84 Engine reassembly - completion and final adjustments

1 Refit the oil feed pipes that connect the carburettor warming system to the lubrication system (if fitted). It is advisable to use new washers at the union joints.
2 Replace the sparking plug after checking that it is gapped at 0.024 inch. Replace also the plug lead and waterproof cover.
3 Replace and tighten the crankcase drain plug. Refill the sump with clean engine oil of the recommended viscosity. The overhead camshaft engines have a capacity of approximately 0.9 litres (just over 1½ Imperial pints), depending on the model. Check with the dipstick and if necessary add oil until the level is correct.

79.1. Holding down studs hold rocker pins captive

79.2. Feed chain and sprocket through tunnel to line up with camshaft

79.3. Full gasket between cylinder barrel and head

79.4. Fit finned top cover and tighten down before timing engine

80.3. Alignment of components for correct timing

80.8. Side covers fit as shown

82.2. Stator plate has outer 'O' ring seal

83.1. Marks on rim of flywheel make timing easy

83.2. Fit outer cover to complete reassembly

83.3. Aligning engine unit with frame

84.1. Oil feed pipes form part of carburettor deicing system

84.1A. Use new washers to prevent leaks at union joints

85 Starting and running the rebuilt engine

1 If the machine is fitted with the carburettor warming system, slacken the upper of the two oil unions of the warming pipes at the cylinder barrel joint. Oil should dribble from this joint very soon after the engine starts; if it does not, stop the engine and check the lubrication system. An overhead camshaft engine is very dependent on a full flow of oil to the cylinder head and overhead camshaft, otherwise very rapid and severe wear will occur.

2 On other models without the carburettor warming system, removal of the rocker box caps will provide evidence of oil circulation.

3 Remember that if a number of new parts have been fitted or if the engine has been rebored, it will be necessary to follow the original running-in instructions so that the new parts have ample opportunity to bed down in a satisfactory manner. Check for oil leaks and/or blowing gaskets before the machine is run on the road.

86 Fault diagnosis - engines

Symptom	Cause	Remedy
Engine will not turn over	Clutch slip	Check and adjust clutch.
	Flat battery or bad battery connection	Recharge or replace battery. Check all connections are clean and tight.
Engine turns over but will not start	No spark at plug	Remove plug and check.
	No fuel reaching engine	Check fuel system.
	Too much fuel reaching engine	Check fuel system.
	Contact breaker gap incorrect, or points dirty	Check contact breaker.
Engine runs but fires unevenly	Ignition and/or fuel system fault	Check systems as though engine would not start.
	Incorrect valve clearances	Check and reset.
	Burnt valves	Check compression. If none, remove cylinder head and examine.
	Blowing cylinder head gasket	Leak should be audible. Lift cylinder head and replace gasket.
	Incorrect ignition timing	Check timing marks for accuracy of setting.
Lack of power	Incorrect ignition timing	See above.
	Fault in fuel system	Check fuel system.
	Incorrect valve clearances	Check and reset tappets.
	Burnt valves	Check compression.
	Blowing cylinder head gasket	See above.
	Badly worn cylinder barrel and/or piston	Examine piston and cylinder barrel. Check with list of tolerances.
High oil consumption	Oil leaks from engine/gear unit	Identify source of leak and rectify.
	Cylinder barrel in need of rebore and o/s piston	Fit new rings and piston after rebore.
	Worn valve guides	Recondition as appropriate.
Excessive mechanical noise	Failure of lubrication system	Stop engine and do not run until fault located.
	Wrong valve clearances	Re-adjust.
	Worn cylinder barrel (piston slap)	Rebore and fit o/s piston.
	Worn big-end bearing (rattle)	Fit new crankshaft assembly.
	Worn crankshaft bearings (rumble)	Fit new journal bearings.

87 Fault diagnosis - gearbox

Symptom	Cause	Remedy
Difficulty in engaging gears	Gear selectors not indexed correctly	Check that screwed pins engage fully with selector drum.
	Gear selector forks bent	Replace selector forks.
Machine jumps out of gear	Worn dogs on ends of gear pinions	Replace worn pinions.
	Selector pawl spring broken	Replace spring.
Kickstarter does not return when engine is turned over or started	Broken or misplaced return spring	Replace spring or tension correctly.
Gear pedal does not return to original position	Ditto	Ditto

Chapter 2 Clutch

Contents

General description ... 1	Clutch - reassembly ... 5
Clutch assembly - dismantling ... 2	Clutch - adjustment ... 6
Clutch - examination and renovation ... 3	Clutch - correct operation ... 7
Clutch operating mechanism - examination and renovation ... 4	Fault diagnosis - clutch ... 8

Specifications

Clutch springs
Number ... 4 or 8, depending on model
Free length ... 19.2 mm (S65 model)
26.8 mm (S90 model)
27.0 mm (C90 model)
Minimum length ... 18.2 mm (S65 model)
26.0 mm (S90 and C90 models)

Inserted clutch plates
Number ... 2 or 3, depending on model
Thickness ... 3.5 mm (S65 model)
2.9 mm (S90 and C90 models)
Minimum thickness ... 2.1 mm (S65 model)
2.4 mm (S90 and C90 models)

1 General description

The clutch is of the multi-plate type having two or three plain plates and two or three inserted plates depending on the model. The clutch is fully automatic in operation (scooter models) and is interconnected with the gear change pedal so that it disengages and re-engages in the correct sequence or is manually operated by the customary handlebar mounted clutch lever, via a flexible control cable (motor cycle models).

2 Clutch assembly - dismantling

The clutch assembly complete is removed by following the procedure detailed in Chapter 1.11. When removed, the clutch can be broken down into its component parts as follows:

1 To aid the dismantling of the clutch it is advisable to make up a compressing tool using a normal sprocket puller. It is possible to dispense with this tool if another pair of hands is available during the dismantling operation.
2 Remove the bronze bush from the centre of the drive gear and use a small screwdriver to prise out the four damper springs from the front of the clutch housing.
3 Use the compressing tool, or with the aid of another pair of hands, compress the clutch plate assembly sufficiently to allow the 101 mm circlip to be removed from its location. Release the pressure and withdraw the bronze bush from the centre of the drive gear, the drive gear, plain clutch plates, inserted clutch plates, clutch pressure plate and the eight clutch springs.

1. Dismantled clutch from S65 model

2.1. Clutch must be depressed to release circlip

Fig. 2.1. Clutch components

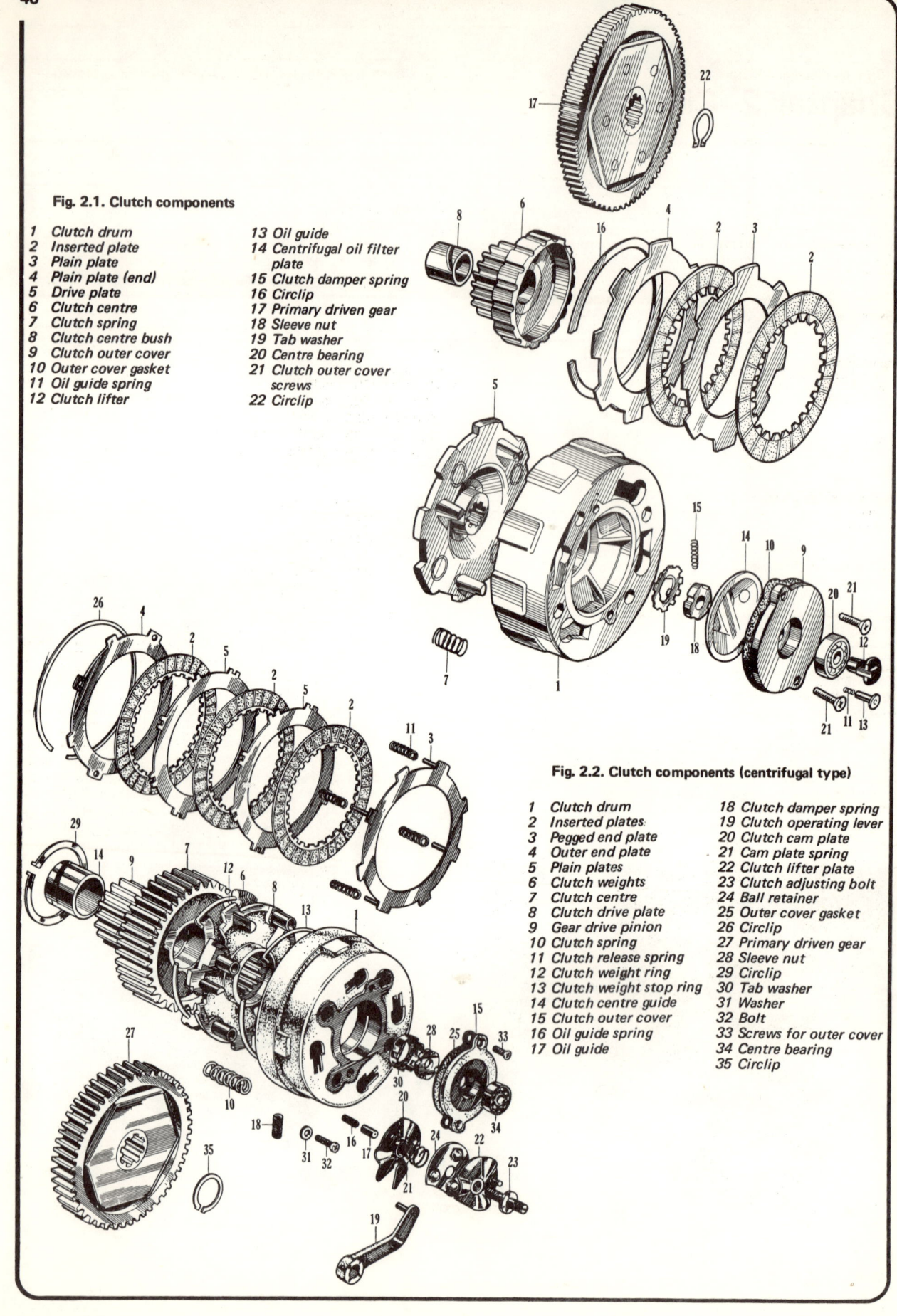

1 Clutch drum
2 Inserted plate
3 Plain plate
4 Plain plate (end)
5 Drive plate
6 Clutch centre
7 Clutch spring
8 Clutch centre bush
9 Clutch outer cover
10 Outer cover gasket
11 Oil guide spring
12 Clutch lifter
13 Oil guide
14 Centrifugal oil filter plate
15 Clutch damper spring
16 Circlip
17 Primary driven gear
18 Sleeve nut
19 Tab washer
20 Centre bearing
21 Clutch outer cover screws
22 Circlip

Fig. 2.2. Clutch components (centrifugal type)

1 Clutch drum
2 Inserted plates
3 Pegged end plate
4 Outer end plate
5 Plain plates
6 Clutch weights
7 Clutch centre
8 Clutch drive plate
9 Gear drive pinion
10 Clutch spring
11 Clutch release spring
12 Clutch weight ring
13 Clutch weight stop ring
14 Clutch centre guide
15 Clutch outer cover
16 Oil guide spring
17 Oil guide
18 Clutch damper spring
19 Clutch operating lever
20 Clutch cam plate
21 Cam plate spring
22 Clutch lifter plate
23 Clutch adjusting bolt
24 Ball retainer
25 Outer cover gasket
26 Circlip
27 Primary driven gear
28 Sleeve nut
29 Circlip
30 Tab washer
31 Washer
32 Bolt
33 Screws for outer cover
34 Centre bearing
35 Circlip

Chapter 2/Clutch assembly

3 Clutch - examination and renovation

1 Check the condition of the clutch drive to ensure none of the teeth are chipped, broken or badly worn.
2 Give the plain and the inserted clutch plates a wash with a paraffin/petrol mix and check that they are not buckled or distorted. Remove all traces of clutch insert debris, otherwise a gradual build-up will affect clutch action.
3 Visual inspection will show whether the tongues of the clutch plates have become burred and whether indentations have formed in the slots with which they engage. Burrs should be removed with a file, which can also be used to dress the slots, provided the depth of the indentations is not too great.
4 Check the thickness of the friction linings in the inserted plates. The recommended serviceable limit is 0.0944 inch (2.4 mm).
If the linings have worn to, or below these limits, the plates should be replaced. Worn linings promote clutch slip.
5 Check also the free length of the clutch springs. The recommended serviceable limit is 1.0236 inch (26.0 mm).
Do not attempt to stretch the springs if they have compressed. They must be replaced when they reach the serviceable limit, as a complete set.

4 Clutch operating mechanism - examination and renovation

CM90, C90 and C70 models:
The automatic clutch fitted to these models is designed so that as the engine speed increases, four specially shaped weights increase their pressure on the clutch plates through being thrown outwards by centrifugal force. Four small diameter compression springs assist the clutch plates to free and four large diameter compression springs supply additional pressure when the weights reach their limit of travel.
A quick acting three-start thread mechanism is incorporated in an extension of the drive gear to apply pressure when the kickstarter is operated, or when the machine is on the over-run.
The clutch is completely disengaged each time the gear operating pedal is moved, through a direct linkage between the gear change lever spindle and the clutch withdrawal mechanism.

C200, S90 and S65 models:
1 Provided the clutch adjustment is correct, as detailed in section 6 of this Chapter, heavy clutch operation can often be traced to a dry, trapped or partially broken operating cable. Check whether the cable has any tight bends or whether it is trapped at any point, allowing the outer covering to become compressed.

3.1. Visual check for damaged teeth on pinion

3.3. Check also for burred tongues on clutch plates

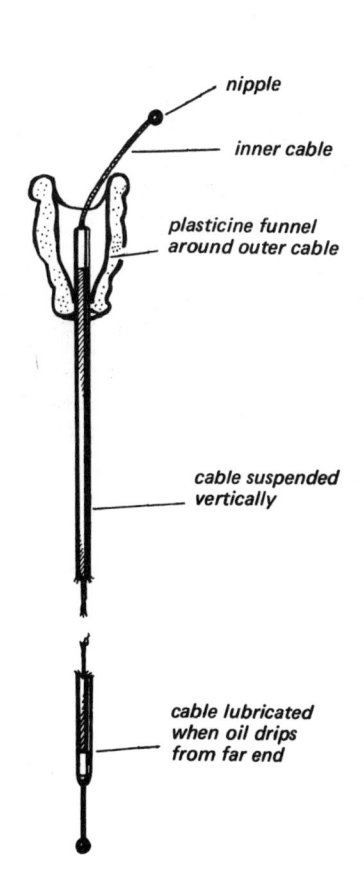

Fig. 2.3. Oiling control cable
- nipple
- inner cable
- plasticine funnel around outer cable
- cable suspended vertically
- cable lubricated when oil drips from far end

2 It is best to remove the cable completely for oiling, so that it can be hung vertically. The accompanying diagram will show how to oil the cable, using a makeshift funnel of paper, plasticine or some similar material. Do not refit the cable to the machine until clean oil issues from the further most end.

3 If any of the inner cable strands are broken or if the outer covering is frayed, broken or compressed, the cable should be replaced. Clutch operation will become particularly heavy if water is able to enter the cable.

5 Clutch - reassembly

1 Reassemble the clutch components by following the dismantling procedure in reverse. A second pair of hands, or the clutch compressing tool is necessary to depress the clutch plates against the spring pressure, whilst the retaining circlip is inserted and correctly located.

2 The built-up clutch is then replaced on the splined end of the right-hand crankshaft, following the engine reassembly procedure given in Chapter 1, section 36. A torque setting of 33.4 ft lbs is recommended for the sleeve nut that retains the clutch in position. Make sure the tab washer is bent over to lock the sleeve nut in position.

6 Clutch - adjustment

CM90, C90 and C70 models:
1 Clutch adjustment is provided by means of an adjustable screw and locknut located in the centre of the clutch cover. Slacken off the 10 mm locknut and turn the adjusting screw firstly in the clockwise direction, to ensure there is no end pressure on the clutch pushrod.

2 Turn the adjusting screw anti-clockwise until pressure can be felt on the end. Turn back (clockwise) for approximately 1/8th of a turn, and tighten the locknut, making sure the screw does not turn. Clutch adjustment should now be correct.

C200, S90 and S65 models:
1 On these models it is first necessary to remove the clutch cover, which is retained by two cross head screws. Adjustment is carried by following the procedure detailed above.

2 The models fitted with a manually-operated clutch have also an adjuster on the clutch cable. Either method of adjustment can be used the adjustment is correct if there is between 0.4 inch - 0.8 inch (1 cm - 2 cm) free play at the handlebar lever before the clutch commences to disengage.

7 Clutch - correct operation

1 Clutch operation on the models fitted with a manually-operated clutch can be checked by using the kickstarter. Clutch slip will make engine starting difficult.

2 With the engine running, disengage the clutch by grasping the clutch lever and see whether the machine starts to move forward or the engine stalls when bottom gear is engaged.

3 The machine should move forward smoothly as the clutch lever is released progressively, whilst increasing the engine speed.

4 Note that these checks cannot be applied to any of the models fitted with an automatic clutch because the special starting mechanism engages when the engine is turned over by the kickstarter.

5.2. Slide complete clutch assembly on end of mainshaft

5.2B. Tighten to recommended torque setting

6.1. Adjustment is effected by centre screw and locknut

8 Fault diagnosis - clutch

Symptom	Cause	Remedy
Engine speed increases but machine does not respond	Clutch slip	Check clutch adjustment for pressure on push rod or free play at handlebar lever. Check depth of linings, also free length of clutch springs. Replace if serviceable limits reached.
Difficulty in engaging gears. Gear changes jerky and machine moves forward, even when clutch is fully withdrawn	Clutch drag	Check clutch adjustment for too much free play.
	Clutch plates worn and/or clutch housing	Check for burrs on clutch plate tongues or indentations in clutch housing slots. Dress with file.
	Clutch assembly loose on crankcase splines	Check tightness of retaining sleeve nut. If loose, fit new tab washer and retighten.
Operating action stiff	Damaged, frayed or trapped control cable	Check cable and replace if necessary. Make sure cable is well lubricated and has no sharp bends.

Chapter 3 Fuel system and carburation

Contents

General description ... 1	Carburettor - dismantling ... 6
Petrol tank - removal and replacement .. 2	Carburettor - adjustments ... 7
Petrol tap - removal and replacement ... 3	Air filter - cleaning ... 8
Carburettor - general description ... 4	Exhaust system - cleaning ... 9
Carburettor - removal ... 5	Fault diagnosis - fuel system and carburation .. 10

Specifications

Fuel tank capacity

S65 model ... 6.5 litre (11.4 Imp. pints) (13.7 U.S. pints)

C70 model ... 4.5 litres (7.9 Imp. pints) (9.5 U.S. pints)

C90 and CM90 models ... 5.5 litres (9.7 Imp. pints) (11.6 U.S. pints)

S90 model ... 7 litres (12.32 Imp. pints) (14.80 U.S. pints)

C200 model ... 8.5 litres (14.8 Imp. pints) (17.9 U.S. pints)

Carburettor

	C200, CM90	S65	C70	C90, S90	
Make	Keihin		(No model		
Type	DPW14H1	PW18X1	number)	PW15HAI, PW2OH or UM20H	
Main jet	95 80	85	75	75	85
Slow running jet	no data currently	38	35	40	38
Throttle valve	available	1.5	012304	2.0	2.5
Jet needle		16305	2.5 mm	16332	18241
Slow running screw		1 to 1½ turns out			

1 General description

The fuel system comprises a fuel tank from which petrol is fed by gravity to the float chamber of the carburettor. The open frame layout of the scooter-type models necessitates the use of a specially-shaped petrol tank that is located immediately below the nose of the dual seat. On these models, the petrol tap is incorporated in the top of the carburettor float chamber.

All machines are fitted with a carburettor of Keihin manufacture, the model depending on the type of machine to which the carburettor is fitted. All carburettors have a manually-operated choke and employ a throttle slide and needle arrangement for controlling the petrol/air mixture administered to the engine.

2 Petrol tank - removal and replacement

1 It is unlikely that the petrol tank will need to be removed except on very infrequent occasions, because it does not restrict access to the engine unit of any of the models. Before the petrol tank can be removed, it is necessary to detach the dual seat.

CM90, C90 and C70 models:

1 Remove the two 10 mm nuts and washers that clamp the rear bracket of the dual seat to the frame. The front of the seat is fitted with a detachable spring-loaded fastener, to permit the seat to be raised for access to the filler cap. If this fastener is undone, the dual seat can be removed from the machine.
2 The petrol tank is attached to the frame by four 10 mm bolts. After the bolts have been removed, the tank can be lifted clear of the frame and the pull-off petrol pipe disconnected. Have available some means of blocking the petrol pipe to impede the flow of petrol, or else drain the tank before it is removed.
3 To replace the tank, reverse this procedure.

C200, S90 and S65 models:

1 Loosen the two domed nuts at the upper end of the rear suspension units and pull the dual seat away from the petrol tank in a rearwards direction. A considerable amount of effort may be needed, especially if the domed nuts have been over-tightened.
2 The petrol tank is attached to the frame by the rear end only, using a 10 mm bolt. Two rubber buffers at the forward end of the frame locate in two slots in the centre channel of the petrol tank.

3 Drain the petrol from the tank and disconnect the pipe that joins the two separate halves.
4 Remove the 10 mm rear fixing bolt, nut and washers.
5 Raise the rear end of the tank slightly and pull rearwards, to detach the rubber buffers from the slots in the centre channel. The tank can now be withdrawn from the frame.
6 To replace the tank, reverse this procedure.

3 Petrol tap - removal and replacement

C200, S90 and S65 models:

Before the petrol tap can be removed from the tank, it is necessary to remove the filter bowl, sealing washer and gauze.
1 The filter bowl is threaded to the petrol tap body and can be removed by using a 10 mm ring or socket spanner.
2 Lift out the synthetic rubber sealing washer and the filter gauze. This will reveal the crosshead screw that retains the tap. A synthetic rubber sealing washer is fitted between the body of the tap and the petrol tank.
3 Remove the two crosshead screws from the plate that retains the tap lever. If the plate and spring washer are removed, the tap lever will be released. The rubber gland washer fitted between the tap body and the tap lever should be renewed, irrespective of whether it appears damaged.
4 During reassembly, the top side of the gland washer should be lightly smeared with vaseline, to aid the smoothness of the tap operation. Do not overtighten any of the components during reassembly, otherwise there is risk of permanent damage to the synthetic rubber washers.

4 Carburettor - general description

Various types of Keihin carburettor are fitted to the Honda 65 cc - 90 cc models, the exact specification depending on the designation of the model. Air is drawn into all the carburettors, via an air filter with a removable element. The conventional throttle slide and needle arrangement works in conjunction with the main jet, to control the amount of petrol/air mixture administered to the engine. There is also a slow running jet with an adjustable air screw, to control idling at low speeds, and a manually-operated choke, to aid cold starting.

5 Carburettor - removal

1 Pull off the synthetic rubber tube connecting the air filter to the carburettor intake, following the procedure detailed in Chapter 1/5, sections 8 - 11. Note that on some models it is necessary to detach also the oil feed pipes from the crankcase and valve rockers. These form part of the heating system to prevent the carburettor from icing dueing cold weather running.
2 Make sure the 'O' ring between the flange of the carburettor and the cylinder head is not lost.

6 Carburettor - dismantling

C200 CM90, S90 and S65 models:

1 Remove the float chamber assembly by prising off the spring clip at the base of the carburettor mixing chamber. A synthetic rubber gasket seals the joint between the float chamber and the carburettor mixing chamber.
2 Remove the hinge pin on which the float assembly pivots. The floats can then be withdrawn and the float needle lifted from its seating.
3 The accompanying diagram shows the location of the main jet, needle jet and slow running jet. The needle jet can be displaced after the jet holder has been removed, by pushing in a downwards direction.
4 Note that a secondary oil feed from the crankcase to the valve rockers is fed through the carburettor body, to prevent icing in cold weather running.

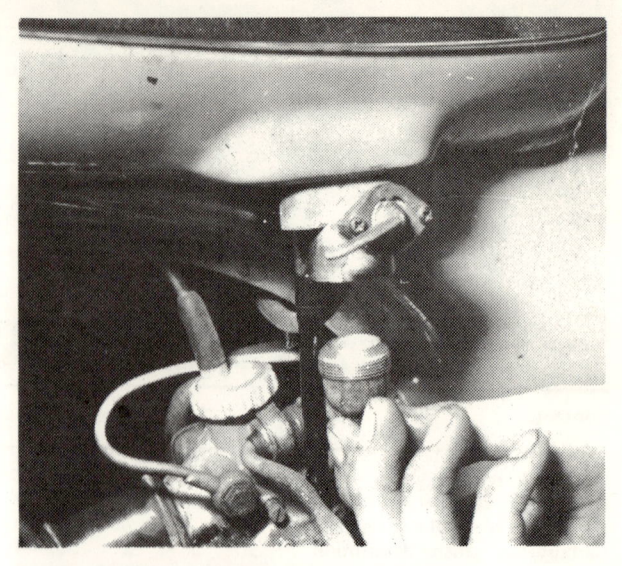

3.1. Filter bowl is threaded to petrol tap body

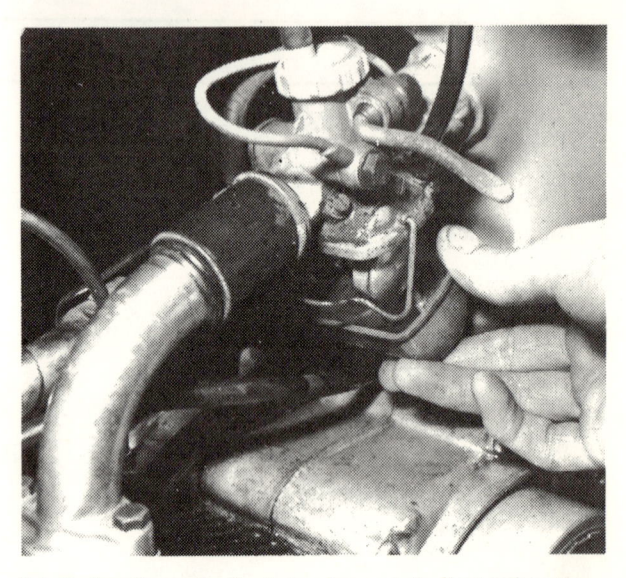

6.1. Spring clip retains float chamber on twin float carburettor

5 Do not use wire or any other thin object to clear a blocked jet because there is a danger of enlarging the hole in the jet, to the detriment of petrol economy. Use compressed air.
6 Further dismantling is not recommended, nor should be necessary.
7 Replace the component parts of the carburettor by reversing this procedure.

C70 and C90 models:

1 Remove the float chamber by unscrewing the two countersunk screws that retain it to the mixing chamber body. An 'O' ring is interposed between the mixing chamber body and the float chamber base, to effect a leaktight seal.
2 To gain access to the petrol filter located in the float chamber top, remove the two crosshead screws that retain the top in position. Immediately below the float chamber top will be found the filter gauze, 'O' ring sealing washer, the filter cap and the seat for the float valve needle. There is also a gasket between the float chamber top and the float chamber, which should not be disturbed unless necessary.
3 The filter assembly can be dismantled for cleaning by unscrewing the float needle seat.

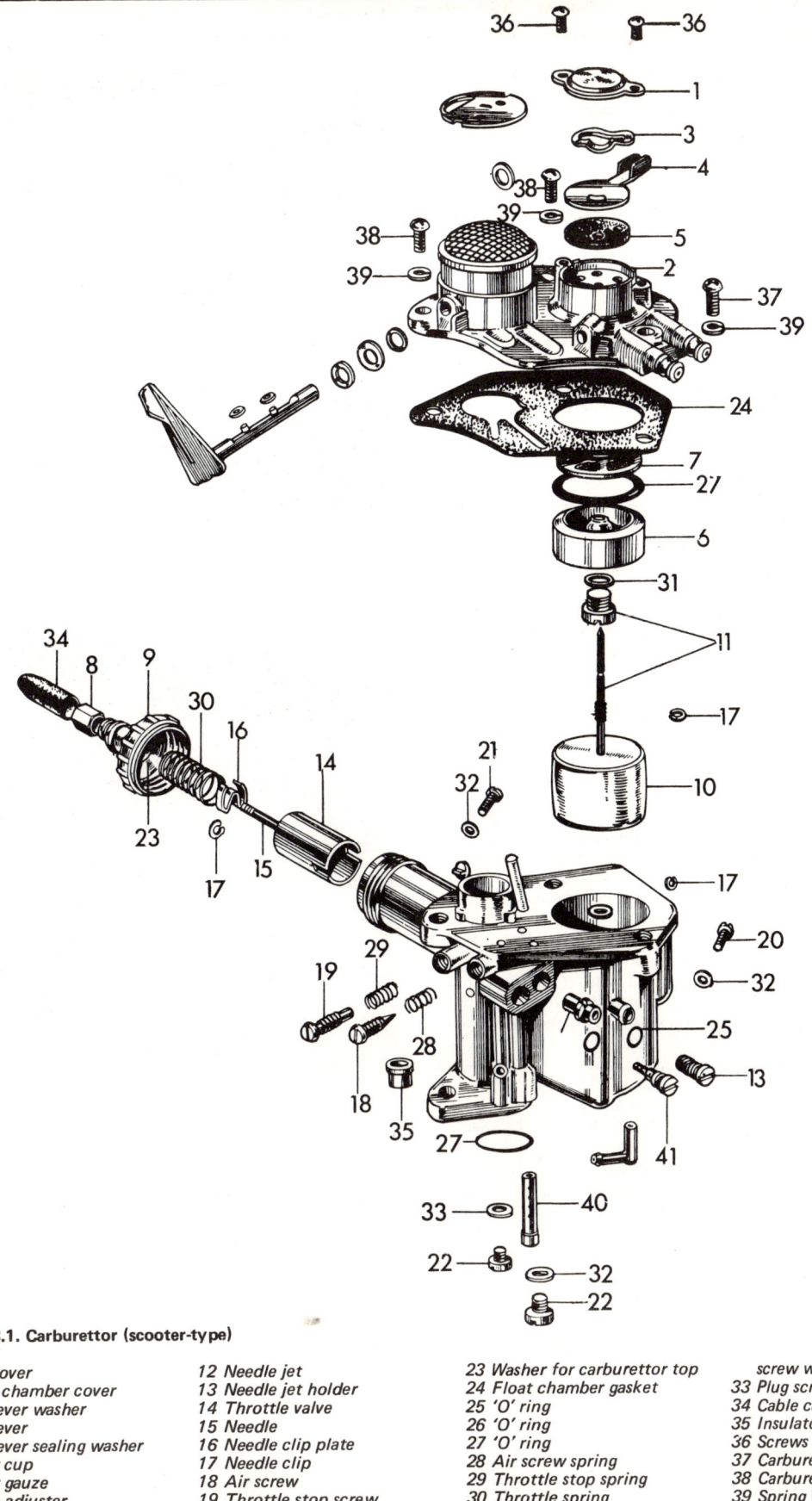

Fig. 3.1. Carburettor (scooter-type)

1 Tap cover	12 Needle jet	23 Washer for carburettor top	screw washers
2 Float chamber cover	13 Needle jet holder	24 Float chamber gasket	33 Plug screw washer
3 Tap lever washer	14 Throttle valve	25 'O' ring	34 Cable cap
4 Tap lever	15 Needle	26 'O' ring	35 Insulator ring
5 Tap lever sealing washer	16 Needle clip plate	27 'O' ring	36 Screws for tap cover
6 Filter cup	17 Needle clip	28 Air screw spring	37 Carburettor body screws
7 Filter gauze	18 Air screw	29 Throttle stop spring	38 Carburettor body screws
8 Cable adjuster	19 Throttle stop screw	30 Throttle spring	39 Spring washer
9 Top of carburettor body	20 Drain screw	31 Washer for float needle seat	40 Main jet
10 Float	21 Drain screw		41 Pilot jet
11 Float needle seat	22 Plug screw	32 Drain screw and plug	

53

4 To dismantle the petrol tap, remove the two crosshead screws that retain the small cap on the float chamber top. Removal of the cap will give access to the tap lever washer, tap lever and packing for the tap. It should not be necessary to dismantle the tap, unless it is leaking.

5 The location of the main jet, needle jet and slow running jet is shown in the attached diagram. These components can be removed for cleaning, which is best accomplished with compressed air. Never use wire or any other thin object to clear a blocket jet because there is danger of enlarging the hole in the jet, to the detriment of petrol economy.

6 Further dismantling is not recommended nor should be necessary. It is unlikely that the butterfly choke assembly will give trouble, unless the screws retaining the butterfly work loose.

7 To reassemble the carburettor, reverse this procedure. If any of the 'O' rings or gaskets show signs of damage, they should be replaced as a matter of course, otherwise there is risk of petrol leakage.

7 Carburettor - adjustments

1 All adjustments should be made when the engine is at normal working temperature.

2 To adjust the slow running, set the throttle stop screw so that the engine runs at a fast tick-over speed.

3 Screw in or out the air screw until the engine runs evenly, without hunting or misfiring. Reduce the engine speed by unscrewing the throttle stop and re-adjust the air screw, if necessary. Do not arrive at a setting where the engine ticks over too slowly, otherwise there is risk that it may stall when the throttle is closed, during normal running.

4 As a rough guide, the air screw should be positioned from one to one and a quarter complete turns out from the fully closed position.

5 The amount of throttle slide cutaway, size of main jet, size of needle jet and size of slow running jet are pre-determined by the manufacturer and should be correct for the model in which they are used. Check with the Specifications, page 51.. The throttle needle position can be varied, by removing and replacing the needle clip. Under normal circumstances, the needle should be positioned in the second or third notch, measured from the top.

6 The slow running jet controls engine speed up to approximately 1/8th throttle and the degree of throttle slide cutaway from 1/8th to ¼ throttle. Thereafter the needle jet takes over, up to ¾ throttle, and the main jet size controls the final ¾ to full throttle. These stages are only approximate; there is a certain amount of overlap.

8 Air filter - cleaning

The air cleaner is found in one of three positions, the exact location depending on the specification of the machine. The scooter-type models house the air filter unit in the tube from the steering head to the bottom bracket, immediately behind the steering head. The S65 model has the air filter assembly in the right hand cover, below the dual seat, and the S90 models utilise a circular cannister mounted crosswise below the fuel tank.

1 To clean the air filter, remove the detachable element and tap it lightly to remove accumulated dust. Blow dry from the inside with compressed air, or brush the exterior with a light brush. Remember the element is made from paper. If it is torn or damaged, fit a replacement.

2 Oil or water will reduce the efficiency of the filter element and may upset the carburettor. Replace any suspect element.

3 It is advisable to replace the element at less than the recommended 6,000 miles if the machine is used in very dusty conditions. The usual signs of a filter element in need of replacement are reduced performance, misfiring and a tendency for the carburation to run rich.

4 On no account should the machine be run without the filter element in place because this will have an adverse effect on carburation.

8. Air filter is behind right-hand cover on S65 model

8A. Removal of cover exposes element

9 Exhaust system - cleaning

Although the exhaust system on a four-stroke does not require such frequent attention as that of a two-stroke, it is nevertheless advisable to inspect the complete system from time to time in order to ensure a build-up of carbon does not cause back pressure. If an engine is nearing the stage where a rebore is necessary, it is advisable to check the exhaust system more frequently. The oily nature of the exhaust gases will cause a more rapid build-up of sludge.

1 The exhaust system complete is removed easily by following the procedure in Chapter 1.5, sections 4 - 5. On the early models, the silencer is a push fit on the end of the exhaust pipe.

2 The cylinder head flange joint relies upon a copper/asbestos washer to effect an airtight seal. If this washer is lost or damaged, air will be admitted and apart from a blowing exhaust, the engine will tend to backfire on the over-run.

3 A 10 mm bolt is in the extreme end of the silencer retains the detachable baffle assembly in position. If this bolt is withdrawn, the baffle tube can be pulled clear of the silencer body, for cleaning.

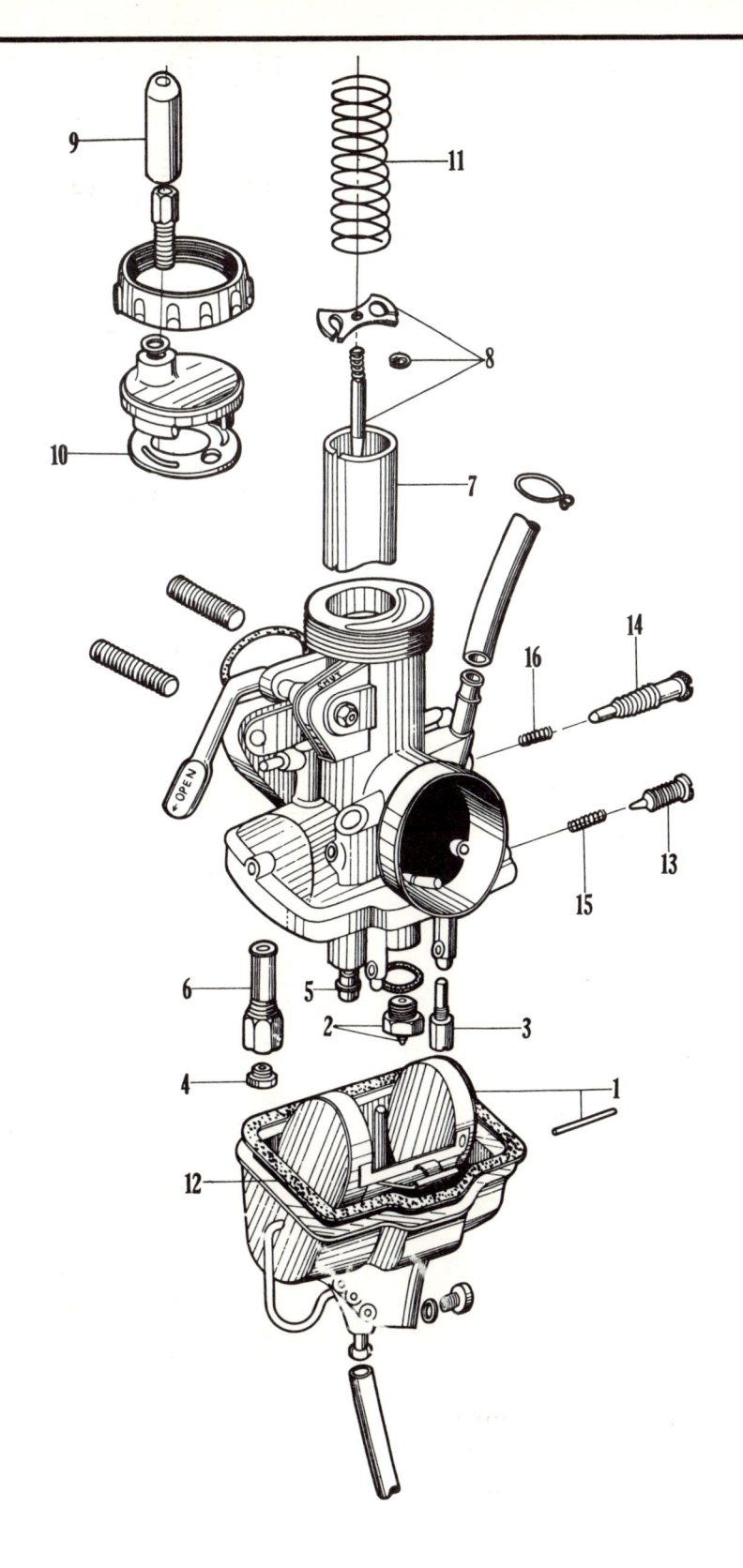

Fig. 3.2. Carburettor (motor cycle type)

1. Float assembly
2. Float needle assembly
3. Pilot jet
4. Main jet
5. Needle jet
6. Needle jet holder
7. Throttle valve
8. Needle, needle clip and needle clip plate
9. Cable cover
10. Carburettor top washer
11. Throttle spring
12. Float chamber gasket
13. Air screw
14. Throttle stop screw
15. Air screw spring
16. Throttle stop spring

4 Tap the baffle to remove loose carbon and work with a wire brush, if necessary. If there is a heavy build-up of carbon or oily sludge, it may be necessary to use a blow lamp to burn out these deposits.

5 Do not run the machine without the baffle tube in position.

Although the changed engine note may give the illusion of greater speed, the net effect will be a marked drop in performance as a result of changes in carburation. There is also risk of prosecution as a result of the excessive noise.

6 When reassembling, make sure the bolt retaining the silencer baffle assembly is replaced and fully tightened.

10 Fault diagnosis - fuel system and carburettor

Symptom	Cause	Remedy
Excessive fuel consumption	Air filter choked, damp or oily	Check, and if necessary replace.
	Fuel leaking from carburettor. Float sticking	Check all unions and gaskets. Float needle seat needs cleaning.
	Badly worn carburettor	Replace.
	Carburettor incorrectly adjusted	Tune and adjust as necessary.
Idling speed too high	Throttle stop screw in too far. Carburettor top loose	Adjust screw. Tighten top.
Engine does not respond to throttle	Back pressure in silencer. Float displaced or punctured	Clean baffles in silencer. Check whether float correctly located or has petrol inside.
Engine dies after running for a short while	Blocked air hole in filler cap	Clean.
	Dirt of water in carburettor	Remove and clean petrol tap filter and float chamber.
General lack of performance	Weak mixture; float needle stuck in seat	Remove float chamber and clean.
	Leak between carburettor and cylinder head	Check joint gasket and replace if necessary.

Chapter 4 Ignition system

Contents

General description ... 1	Condenser - removal and replacement ... 6
Flywheel generators - checking output.. ... 2	Ignition timing - checking and resetting ... 7
Ignition coil - checking ... 3	Automatic advance unit - locating and checking action ... 8
Contact breaker - adjustment ... 4	Sparking plugs - checking and resetting gap ... 9
Contact breaker points - removal, renovation and replacement 5	Fault diagnosis - ignition system ... 10

Specifications

Sparking plugs

	C200, CM90	S65	C70	C90	S90
Make	NGK				
Type	D6H / D6HW	C7HS	C7HS	D6HW/S	D6HW
Make	Champion				
Type	P-7 / P-7	2-10	2-10	P-7	P-7

1 General description

The spark that is necessary to ignite the petrol/air mixture in the combustion chamber is derived from either a flywheel magneto generator attached to the crankshaft of the engine or a battery and coil, depending on the type of generator fitted. Both systems require a contact breaker assembly to determine the precise moment at which the spark will occur; as the points separate the circuit is broken and a high tension voltage is developed across the point of the sparking plug which jumps the air gap and ignites the mixture.

When the engine is running, the surplus voltage produced by the generator is converted into direct current by the rectifier and used to charge the battery. In systems where reliance on the battery is necessary for the initial start-up, there is provision for an 'emergency start' procedure if the battery is fully discharged. The generator provides a small amount of current for the ignition circuit, if there is no additional electrical load. Immediately the engine starts, the battery commences to charge and within a very short time the normal ignition circuit is restored. This latter system applies to models fitted with an electric starter only.

Generator output does not correspond directly to engine rpm and is regulated automatically, obviating the need for a voltage regulator. All the coils in the system are brought into play only if there is a heavy electrical load, such as when all the lights are used during night time running.

2 Flywheel generators - checking output

The output from either of the two types of generator used can be checked only with specialised test equipment of the multi-meter type. It is unlikely that the average owner/rider will have access to this equipment or instruction in its use. In consequence, if the performance of a generator is suspect, it should be checked by a Honda agent or an auto-electrical expert.

3 Ignition coil - checking

The ignition coil is a sealed unit, designed to give long service. It is located within the main spine of the frame assembly. If a weak spark and difficult starting cause its performance to be suspect, it should be tested by a Honda agent or an auto-electrical expert. A faulty coil must be replaced; it is not practicable to effect a repair.

4 Contact breaker - adjustment

All models except S65:

1 To gain access to the contact breaker assembly, remove the two crosshead screws that retain the circular cover plate on the left hand cylinder head side cover, and remove the cover plate and gasket.
2 Rotate the engine until the contact breaker points are in the fully-open position. Examine the faces of the contacts. If they are pitted or burnt it will be necessary to remove them for further attention, as described in section 4.
3 Adjustment is carried out by slackening the two screws that hold the fixed contact breaker plate and moving the plate until there is sufficient clearance for a 0.014 inch feeler gauge to be inserted between the two contacts. Make sure the contacts are fully-open when this adjustment is made, otherwise a false reading will be obtained which will affect the ignition timing. The feeler gauge should be a good sliding fit.
4 Tighten the fixed contact plate screws and recheck the gap.
5 Before replacing the cover plate, place a very light smear of grease on the contact breaker cam, making sure none reaches the contacts.

S65 model only:

1 It is necessary to remove the left hand crankcase cover complete to gain access to the contact breaker points, which will be found within the flywheel magneto generator. A cutaway in

the flywheel rotor permits access when the contact breaker points are in the fully-open position.
2 Adjustment is carried out by following the procedure detailed for the other model as above.
3 Should it be necessary to remove the contact breaker points for further attention or replacement, it will be necessary to withdraw the flywheel magneto generator from the crankshaft, following the procedure given in Chapter 1/7.

5 Contact breaker points - removal, renovation and replacement

1 If the contact breaker points are burned pitted or badly worn, they should be removed for dressing. If it is necessary to remove a substantial amount of material before the faces can be restored, the points should be replaced.
2 To remove the contact breaker points, slacken and remove the nut at the end of the moving contact return spring. Remove the spring washer and plain washer and detach the spring. Note that an insulating washer is located beneath the spring, to prevent the electrical current from being earthed.
3 Remove the spring clip from the moving contact pivot and the insulating washer. Withdraw the moving contact, which is integral with the fibre rocker arm.
4 Remove the screws that retain the fixed contact plate and withdraw the plate complete with contact.
5 The points should be dressed with an oilstone or fine emery cloth. Keep them absolutely square during the dressing operation, otherwise they will make angular contact when they are replaced and will quickly burn away.
6 Replace the contacts by reversing the dismantling procedure. Take particular care to replace the insulating washers in the correct sequence, otherwise the points will be isolated electrically and the ignition system will not function.

6 Condenser - removal and replacement

1 A condenser is included in the contact breaker circuitry to prevent arcing across the contact breaker points as they separate. It is connected in parallel with the points and if a fault develops, ignition failure will occur.
2 If the engine is difficult to start or if misfiring occurs, it is possible that the condenser has failed. To check, separate the contact breaker points by hand whilst the ignition is switched on. If a spark occurs across the points and they have a blackened or burnt appearance, the condenser can be regarded as unserviceable.
3 It is not possible to check the condenser without the necessary test equipment. It is best to fit a replacement condenser and observe the effect on engine performance, especially in view of its low cost.
4 To remove the condenser, withdraw the uppermost fixing screw and slacken the nut that clamps the metal strip attached to the base of the condenser. This strip is slotted, to aid removal.
5 Reassemble by reversing the procedure, making sure the insulating washer remains between the strip and the base of the condenser and the plate to which it is clamped. If this precaution is overlooked, the condenser may be isolated electrically and arcing at the points will re-occur.

7 Ignition timing - checking and re-setting

1 If the ignition timing is correct, the contact breaker points will be about to separate when the 'F' line scribed on the rotor of the flywheel coincides exactly with an arrow or an indentation or similar scribe mark on the left hand crankcase casting. As a check, it should be possible to slide a 0.001 inch feeler gauge between the points, when these timing marks coincide. The 'T' line indicates when the piston is at top dead centre (TDC).

2 Before checking the ignition timing, always make sure the contact breaker gap is correct. If the gap is altered after the timing has been checked, some variation of the accuracy of the ignition timing is inevitable.
3 If the timing is incorrect, the contact breaker gap should be either increased or decreased until the points commence to separate as the timing marks coincide. It is not possible to adjust the position of the stator plate on the S65 model.
4 In the case of other models, the plate holding the complete contact breaker assembly is slotted, to permit a limited range of adjustment. If the two crosshead retaining screws are slackened a little, the plate can be turned until the points commence to separate, and then locked in this position by tightening the screws.
5 After checking the timing, rotate the engine and check again before replacing the covers. The accuracy of the ignition timing is critical in terms of both engine performance and petrol consumption. Even a small error in setting can have a noticeable effect.

8 Automatic advance unit - location and checking action

1 Fixed ignition timing is of little advantage as the engine speed increases and provision is made to advance the timing by centrifugal means, using a balance weight assembly located behind the contact breaker assembly or within the rotor of the flywheel magneto generator (S65 model). A check is not needed unless the action of the unit is in doubt.
2 To check the action of the unit it is first necessary to withdraw the contact breaker assembly complete or withdraw the rotor of the flywheel magneto generator (S65 model). Refer to Chapter 1.7 for the dismantling procedure, commencing with 4.
3 The counterweights of the automatic advance unit should return to their normal position with smooth action when they are spread apart with the fingers and released. A visual inspection will show signs of damage or broken springs.
4 It is unlikely that the automatic advance unit will need to be dismantled, unless replacement parts have to be fitted.

9 Sparking plug - checking and resetting gap

1 A 10 mm NGK sparking plug is fitted to all 65 cc - 90 cc models as standard, the grade depending on the model designation. Refer to the Specifications section heading this Chapter for the recommended grades.
2 All models use a sparking plug with a 12.7 mm reach which should be gapped at 0.024 inch. Always use the grade of plug recommended or the exact equivalent in another manufacturer's range.
3 Check the gap at the plug points during every six monthly or 3,000 mile service. To reset the gap, bend the outer electrode to bring it closer to the central electrode and check that a 0.024 inch feeler gauge can be inserted. Never bend the central electrode, otherwise the insulator will crack, causing engine damage if particles fall in whilst the engine is running.
4 The condition of the sparking plug electrodes and insulator can be used as a reliable guide to engine operating conditions. See accompanying diagrams.
5 Always carry a spare sparking plug of the correct grade. In the rare event of a plug failure it will enable the engine to be restarted.
6 Never over-tighten a sparking plug, otherwise there is risk of stripping the threads from the cylinder head, particularly those cast in light alloy. The plug should be sufficiently tight to seat firmly on the copper sealing washer. Use a spanner that is a good fit, otherwise the spanner may slip and break the insulator.
7 Make sure the plug insulating cap is a good fit and free from cracks. This cap contains the suppressor that eliminates radio and TV interference.

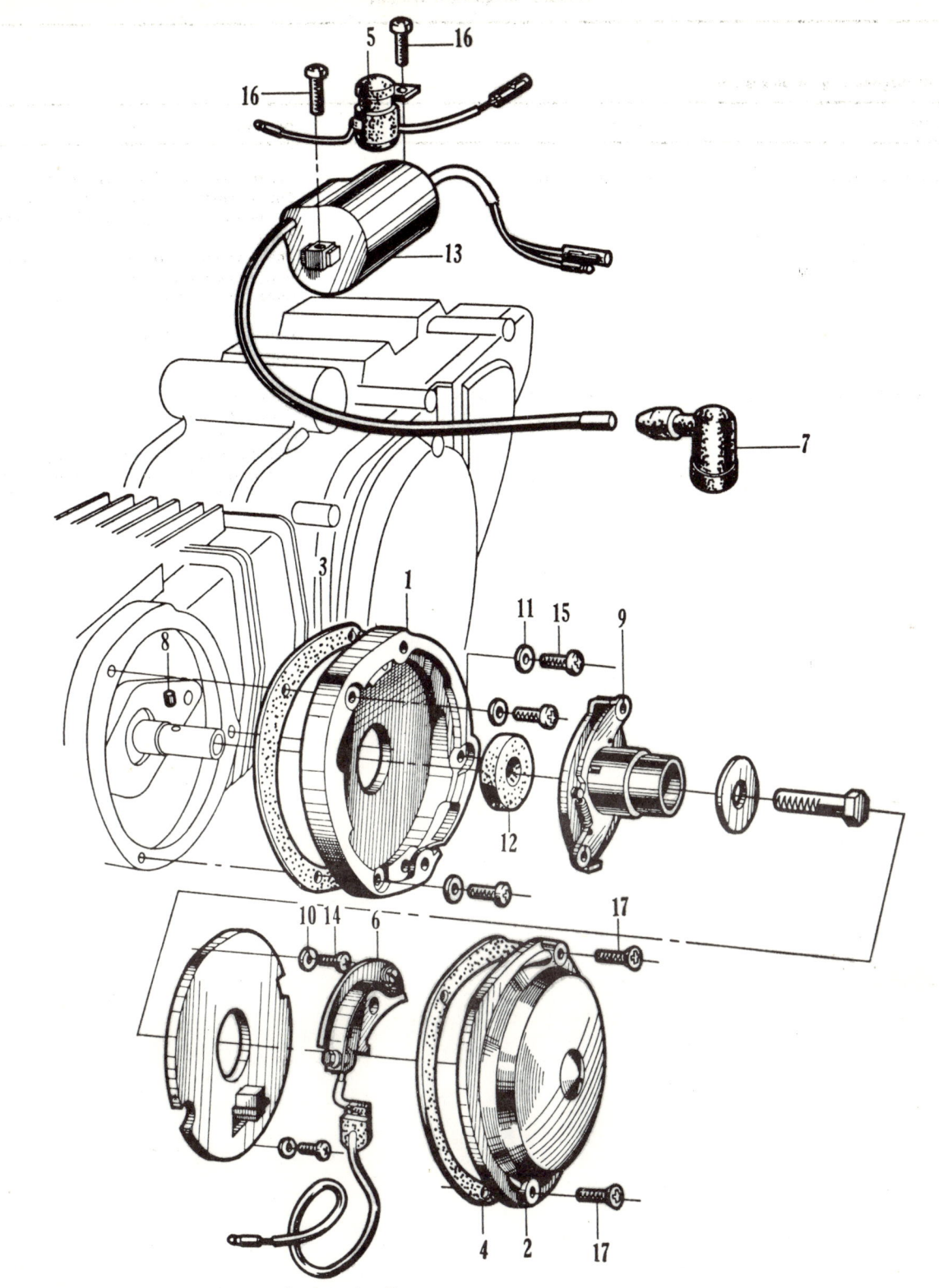

Fig. 4.1. Contact breaker assembly (cylinder head)

1 Base plate
2 Contact breaker cover
3 Base plate cover gasket
4 Contact breaker cover gasket
5 Condenser
6 Contact breaker points
7 Sparking plug cap
8 Dowel pin for advance/retard mechanism
9 Advance/retard mechanism
10 Washer
11 Sealing washers
12 Oil seal
13 Ignition coil
14 Cross head screws
15 Cross head screws for contact breaker assembly
16 Cross head screws for ignition coil
17 Cross head screws for contact breaker cover

Note: The 65 cc and 70 cc engines have the contact breaker assembly within the flywheel magneto generator, on the left-hand side of the engine

10 Fault diagnosis - ignition system

Symptom	Cause	Remedy
Engine will not start	No spark at plug	Try replacement plug if gap correct. Check whether contact breaker points are opening and closing, also whether they are clean. Check whether points arc when separated. If so, replace condenser. Check ignition switch and ignition coil. Battery discharged. Switch off all lights and use emergency start.
Engine starts but runs erratically	Intermittent or weak spark	Try replacement plug. Check whether points are arcing. If so, replace condenser. Check accuracy of ignition timing. Low output from flywheel magneto generator or imminent breakdown of ignition coil.

Chapter 5 Frame and forks

Contents

General description	1
Front forks - removal from frame	2
Front forks - dismantling	3
Steering head bearings - examination and renovation	4
Steering head lock	5
Frame assembly - inspection and renovation	6
Swinging arm rear fork - dismantling, inspection and reassembly	7
Rear suspension units - dismantling and inspection	8
Centre stand - inspection	9
Footrests - inspection and renovation	10
Speedometer - removal and replacement	11
Speedometer cable - inspection and maintenance	12
Speedometer drive gearbox - location and inspection	13
Dualseat - removal	14
Cleaning the plastics mouldings	15
Cleaning - general	16
Fault diagnosis - frame and forks	17

1 General description

Two types of frame are used for the 65 cc - 90 cc models, a scooter-type 'open' frame and a motorcycle frame. Both frame units are of the reinforced spine type, having no front down tube to the bottom bracket. Forks of the bottom link type, with hydraulically-damped spring suspension units are fitted to all models, with the exception of the S90 series. These latter models have telescopic forks of conventional design that contain provision for hydraulic damping. All models have swinging arm rear suspension, controlled by hydraulically-damped spring units.

2 Front forks - removal from frame

CM90, C90 and C70 models:

1 It is extremely unlikely that the front forks will need to be removed from the frame as a unit, unless the steering head bearings give trouble or the forks are damaged in an accident.
2 Before the handlebars can be removed, it is necessary to detach the front of the headlamp and disconnect all the electrical leads by means of their snap connectors. The wires are colour coded, to make re-connection easy.
3 Uncouple the speedometer drive cable and remove the front brake cable from the handlebar lever.
4 Disconnect the throttle cable by unscrewing the top from the carburettor body. Detach the cable end from the throttle slide.
5 Slacken and remove the two 8 mm nuts together with their washers, from the underside of the handlebar fairing. The handlebars can now be removed, complete with the fairing, speedometer and handlebar controls.
6 Remove the moulded headlamp casing by withdrawing the crosshead screw below the horn grille and the two 6 mm nuts and washers inside the headlamp shell.
7 Place a stand beneath the engine to raise the front wheel well clear of the ground and remove the front brake cable and speedometer drive cable from the wheel hub.
8 Withdraw the split pin from the front wheel spindle nut and remove the nut and washer. The front wheel spindle can now be pulled out, releasing the wheel complete with brake assembly.
9 Remove the top bridge of the fork by unscrewing the steering head stem sleeve nut and the two 8 mm bolts and washers.

10 Unscrew the steering head column nut, using a 36 mm 'C' spanner to engage with the slots. The complete fork assembly can now be withdrawn from the frame by pulling it away from the bottom end of the steering column. Make provision for catching the loose ball bearings that will be released as the cup and cone steering head bearings separate.

C200 and S65 models:

1 It is necessary to follow a slightly different procedure with these models, which have conventional handlebars. The handlebars are attached to a lower cover by split clamps, that acts also as a speedometer mounting. They bed down on a rubber pad, to isolate engine vibration.
2 To remove the handlebars, it is necessary to disconnect all the electrical leads within the headlamp shell, the speedometer drive cable and also the cables from the handlebar controls. The handlebar can then be removed by withdrawing the bolts from the split clamps and pulling them free. Remove also the plate on which the handlebars seat.
3 After the handlebars have been removed, the dismantling procedure detailed above can be followed, commencing with section 7. Note that it is necessary to remove also the nut and bolt from the torque arm before the front wheel can be detached.

S90 model only:

1 These models are fitted with telescopic forks, necessitating a different method of approach.
2 Commence operations by detaching the electrical connections within the headlamp shell, where they are joined by snap connectors. Remove also the speedometer drive cable and the control cables from the handlebar controls and finally the headlamp shell.
3 Remove the handlebars by unscrewing the bolts holding the split clamps.
4 Place a stand beneath the engine to raise the front wheel well clear of the ground and remove the front brake cable and speedometer drive cable from the hub.
5 Remove the nut and bolt from the torque arm and also the split pin from the front wheel spindle nut. If the nut and washer are removed, the spindle can be pulled out, releasing the front wheel complete with brake assembly.
6 Unscrew the 29 mm steering head nut at the top of the front

fork yoke and the two nuts, one at the top of each fork leg. The yoke can now be withdrawn, to give access to the steering head column nut.

7 Unscrew the steering head column nut, using a 36 mm 'C' spanner and withdraw the complete fork unit from the bottom of the steering head column. Make provision for catching the loose ball bearings that will be released as the cup and cone steering head bearings separate.

3 Front forks - dismantling

C200, S65 and CM90 models:

1 To remove the suspension units, withdraw the upper and lower pivot bolts. The former is the large bolt with a circular, chromium plated head, located at the point where the front mudguard bridge is attached to the fork blades. The latter is rearmost bolt at the base of the forks, in line with the bottom mudguard stay.

2 The suspension units can now be removed from within the fork blades, leaving only the rubber 'bump' stop in position. The bump stop need not be removed unless it is damaged or perished, in which case it can be withdrawn by removing the 8 mm bolt that passes through it. The bump stop provides the means of cushioning the fork action during full deflection, to prevent the forks from bottoming.

3 To detach the bottom link from the suspension units, remove the pivot bolt and nut. Provided the machine has been greased regularly it is unlikely that either the pivot bolt or the bush within the pivot eye will require attention. If play is evident, both components will need to be replaced. The bush is a press fit in the pivot eye; the replacement bush can be used to press out the old bush by using a drawbolt and distance piece arrangement. When replacing a bush, make sure the grease hole lines up with the grease nipple.

4 The suspension units can be dismantled partially if it is desired to remove the spring. Hold the uppermost end of the unit in a vice and slacken the locknut by placing a spanner across the flats. The complete end casting can be unscrewed and withdrawn from the damper rod, together with the locknut. The suspension spring can then be withdrawn and if necessary replaced. Note that it is of the two-rate type, in which the spring coils at the lower end are closer together. Replace if the free length is below 120 mm.

5 Note that the damper units are sealed and cannot be dismantled further. If the units leak or if the damping action is lost, replacement of the unit is the only answer.

C90 and C70 models:

6 Although the front fork layout is basically similar to that of the earlier models, certain detail improvements necessitate revision of the dismantling procedure. Use these notes in conjunction with the procedure detailed previously.

7 The later-type suspension units do not use an upper eye for attachment to the forks by a through bolt. Instead, the upper end of the suspension unit is attached to an abutment in each fork leg using a 7 mm locknut and a 6 mm pin. If the pin is removed the 7 mm locknut unscrewed and the cap washer and rubber washer removed, each suspension unit can be withdrawn after releasing the bottom pivot bolt.

8 The pivot bearing of the bottom link arm has a dust seal washer and cap, which is clenched in position. The dust cap and seal must be removed before the pivot bush can be replaced.

9 The spring of the suspension unit can be released by removing the locknut and cap that abuts on the end of the spring.

S90 model only:

1 These models are fitted with telescopic forks and require a quite different dismantling procedure. It is unlikely that a complete strip-down will be necessary unless the forks lose their damping action or if the fork bushes are badly worn. It is not practicable to repair forks that have been damaged in an accident.

2 To commence the dismantling procedure, remove the two 6 mm bolts that retain the front mudguard to each fork leg. Detach the front mudguard complete.

3 Pull off the upper fork shrouds, to which the headlamp brackets are attached.

4 Remove the two 8 mm pinch bolts that clamp the fork legs in the bottom yoke. Before the fork legs are removed, mark them so that they are replaced in approximately the same position. Withdraw them from the bottom of the yoke.

5 The bottom yoke can now be removed from the steering head by unscrewing the steering head sleeve nut with a 36 mm 'C' spanner. Make provision for catching the loose ball bearings that will be released as the cup and cone steering head bearings separate.

6 If it is necessary to dismantle each fork leg, they should be drained of their oil content by removing the 8 mm drain plug at the base. Remove the lower fork shroud seat packing the shroud seat itself and the rubber gaiter. The fork spring and the spring guide can now be withdrawn.

7 Remove the 37 mm internal circlip and withdraw the fork tubes from the lower forklegs, after separating the piston and limit rings from the bottom of each tube. Access is now available to the fork bushes.

8 It is good policy to renew the oil seal located immediately below the 37 mm circlip whilst the fork legs are dismantled, taking care the new seal is not damaged during reassembly. Make sure all parts of the damper unit are scrupulously clean.

4 Steering head bearings - examination and renovation

1 Before commencing to reassemble the forks, inspect the steering head races. The ball bearing tracks should be polished and free from indentations or cracks. If signs of wear or damage are evident, the cups and cones must be replaced. They are a tight push fit and need to be drifted out of position.

2 Ball bearings are cheap. Each race has 21 x 3/16 inch ball bearings, which should be replaced if the originals are marked or discoloured. To hold the steel balls in position during the re-attachment of the forks, pack the bearings with grease.

3 The forks are reassembled and attached to the frame by following a reversal of the procedure listed under the different model headings. Do not over-tighten the steering head bearings, otherwise the handling characteristics of the machine will be affected. It is possible to over-tighten and create a load of several tons on the steering head bearings, even though the handlebars appear to turn with relative ease. As a guide, only very slight pressure should be needed to start the front wheel turning to either side under its own weight, when it is raised clear of the ground. Check also that the bearings are not too slack; there should be no discernable movement of the forks, in the fore and aft direction.

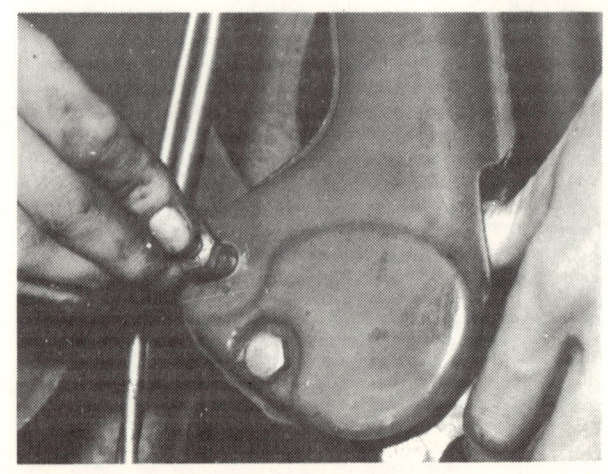

3.1. Remove rear most bolt to release bottom link

3.1A. Bolt acts also as mudguard attachment point

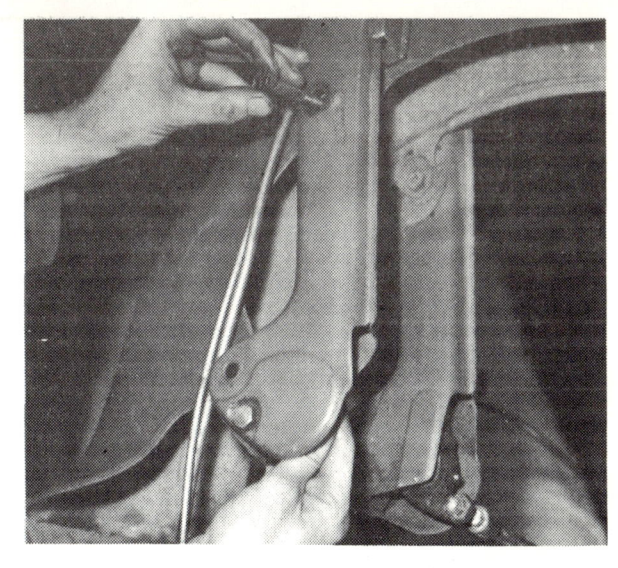

3.1B. Large headed bolt is top mounting for suspension unit

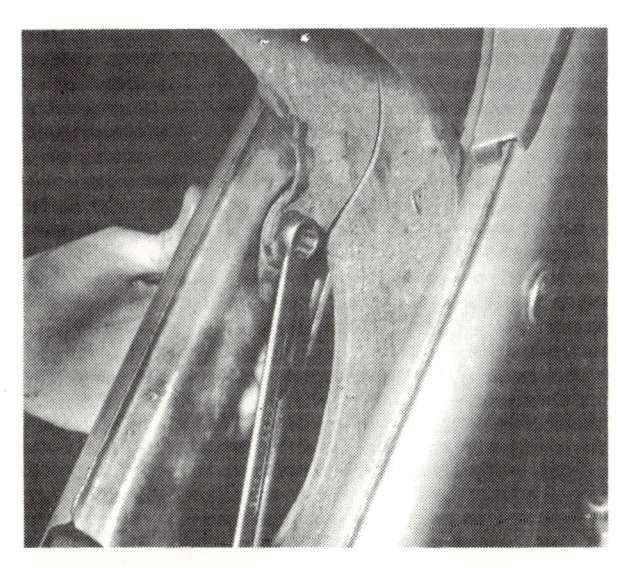

3.1C. This bolt also provides mudguard mounting point

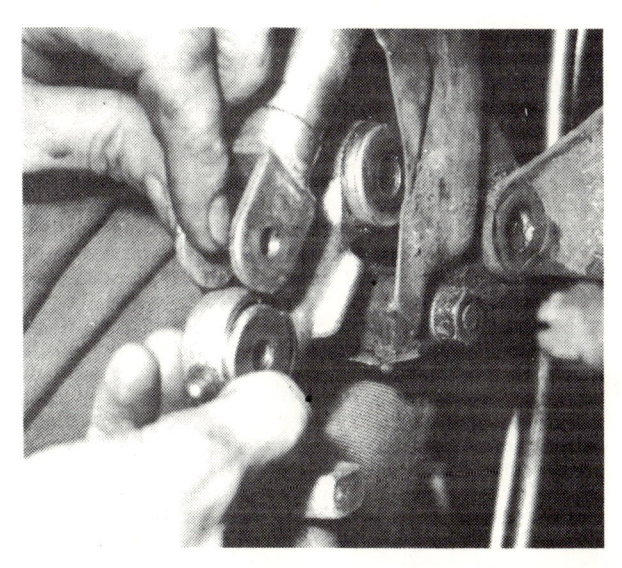

3.3. Bottom link is removed by withdrawing pivot screw

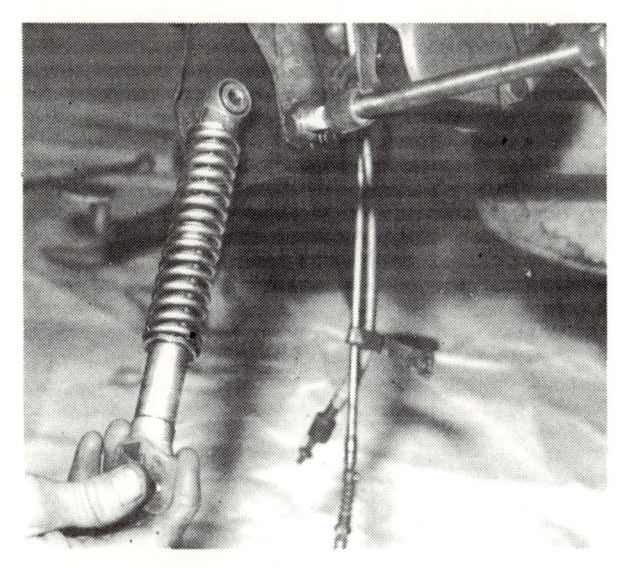

3.4. The complete suspension unit, prior to further dismantling

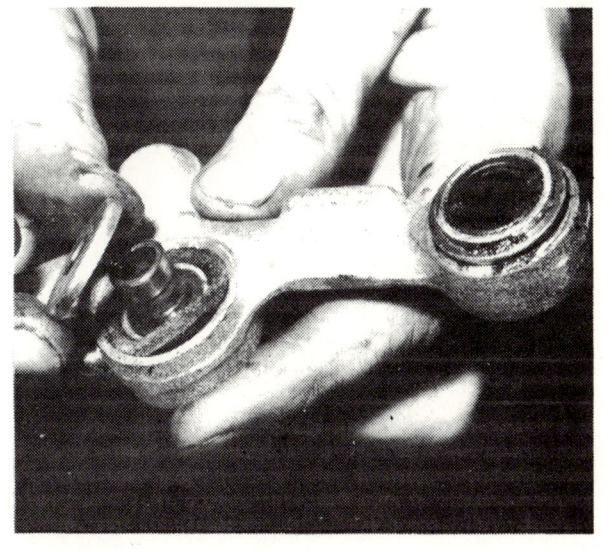

3.8. Dust cap and felt washer seal bearing

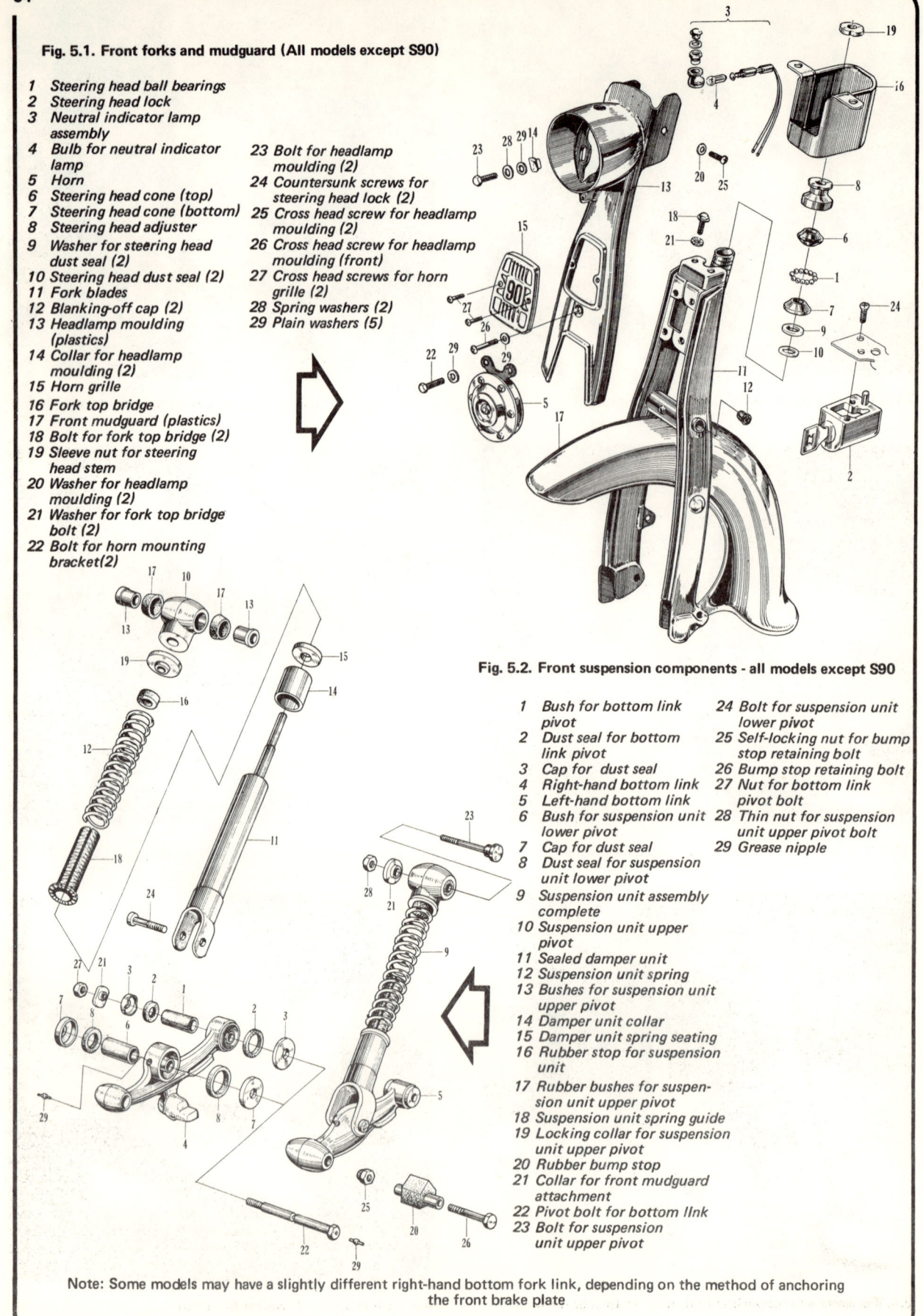

Fig. 5.1. Front forks and mudguard (All models except S90)

1. Steering head ball bearings
2. Steering head lock
3. Neutral indicator lamp assembly
4. Bulb for neutral indicator lamp
5. Horn
6. Steering head cone (top)
7. Steering head cone (bottom)
8. Steering head adjuster
9. Washer for steering head dust seal (2)
10. Steering head dust seal (2)
11. Fork blades
12. Blanking-off cap (2)
13. Headlamp moulding (plastics)
14. Collar for headlamp moulding (2)
15. Horn grille
16. Fork top bridge
17. Front mudguard (plastics)
18. Bolt for fork top bridge (2)
19. Sleeve nut for steering head stem
20. Washer for headlamp moulding (2)
21. Washer for fork top bridge bolt (2)
22. Bolt for horn mounting bracket (2)
23. Bolt for headlamp moulding (2)
24. Countersunk screws for steering head lock (2)
25. Cross head screw for headlamp moulding (2)
26. Cross head screw for headlamp moulding (front)
27. Cross head screws for horn grille (2)
28. Spring washers (2)
29. Plain washers (5)

Fig. 5.2. Front suspension components - all models except S90

1. Bush for bottom link pivot
2. Dust seal for bottom link pivot
3. Cap for dust seal
4. Right-hand bottom link
5. Left-hand bottom link
6. Bush for suspension unit lower pivot
7. Cap for dust seal
8. Dust seal for suspension unit lower pivot
9. Suspension unit assembly complete
10. Suspension unit upper pivot
11. Sealed damper unit
12. Suspension unit spring
13. Bushes for suspension unit upper pivot
14. Damper unit collar
15. Damper unit spring seating
16. Rubber stop for suspension unit
17. Rubber bushes for suspension unit upper pivot
18. Suspension unit spring guide
19. Locking collar for suspension unit upper pivot
20. Rubber bump stop
21. Collar for front mudguard attachment
22. Pivot bolt for bottom link
23. Bolt for suspension unit upper pivot
24. Bolt for suspension unit lower pivot
25. Self-locking nut for bump stop retaining bolt
26. Bump stop retaining bolt
27. Nut for bottom link pivot bolt
28. Thin nut for suspension unit upper pivot bolt
29. Grease nipple

Note: Some models may have a slightly different right-hand bottom fork link, depending on the method of anchoring the front brake plate

65

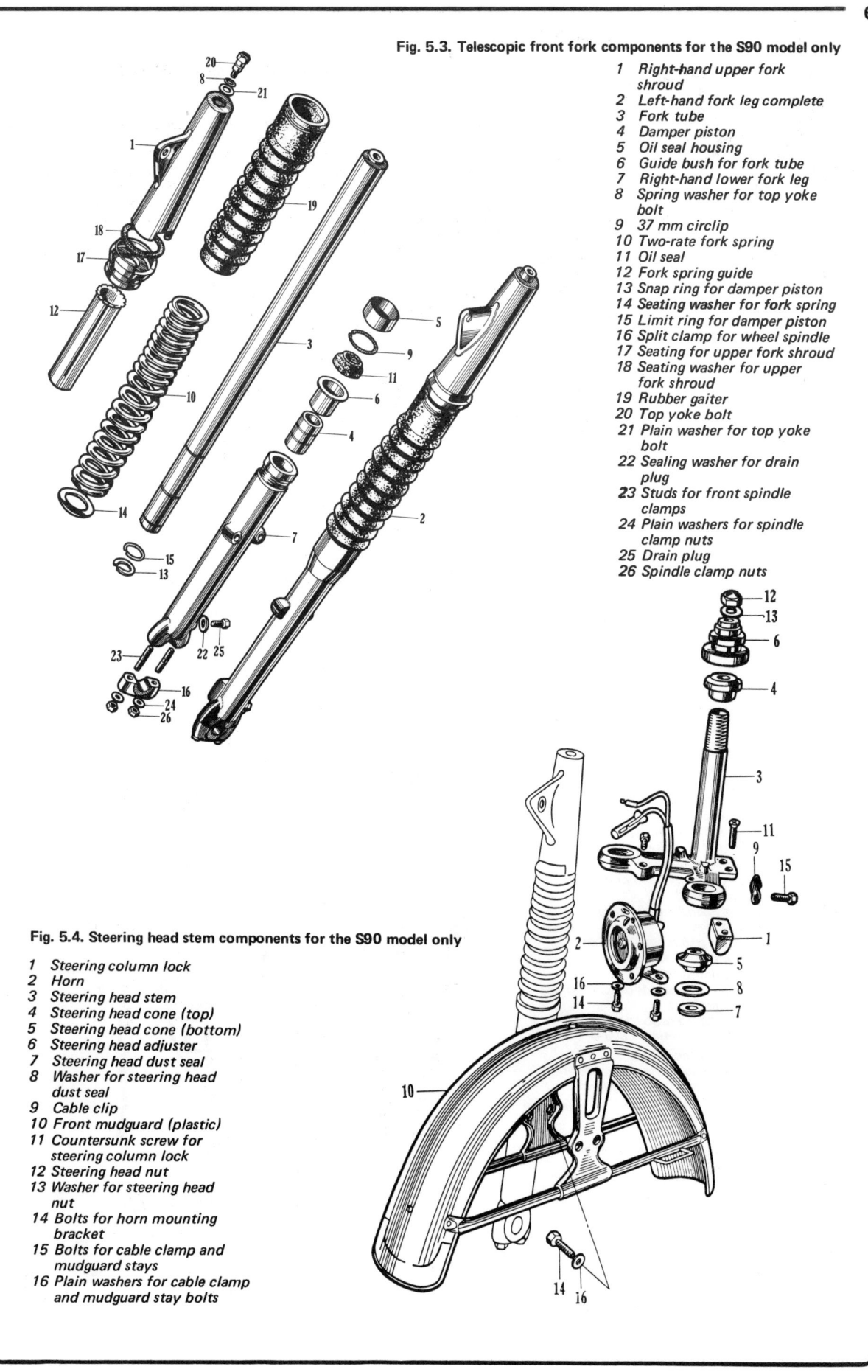

Fig. 5.3. Telescopic front fork components for the S90 model only

1. Right-hand upper fork shroud
2. Left-hand fork leg complete
3. Fork tube
4. Damper piston
5. Oil seal housing
6. Guide bush for fork tube
7. Right-hand lower fork leg
8. Spring washer for top yoke bolt
9. 37 mm circlip
10. Two-rate fork spring
11. Oil seal
12. Fork spring guide
13. Snap ring for damper piston
14. Seating washer for fork spring
15. Limit ring for damper piston
16. Split clamp for wheel spindle
17. Seating for upper fork shroud
18. Seating washer for upper fork shroud
19. Rubber gaiter
20. Top yoke bolt
21. Plain washer for top yoke bolt
22. Sealing washer for drain plug
23. Studs for front spindle clamps
24. Plain washers for spindle clamp nuts
25. Drain plug
26. Spindle clamp nuts

Fig. 5.4. Steering head stem components for the S90 model only

1. Steering column lock
2. Horn
3. Steering head stem
4. Steering head cone (top)
5. Steering head cone (bottom)
6. Steering head adjuster
7. Steering head dust seal
8. Washer for steering head dust seal
9. Cable clip
10. Front mudguard (plastic)
11. Countersunk screw for steering column lock
12. Steering head nut
13. Washer for steering head nut
14. Bolts for horn mounting bracket
15. Bolts for cable clamp and mudguard stays
16. Plain washers for cable clamp and mudguard stay bolts

Fig. 5.5. Handlebar fitment - S90 model only

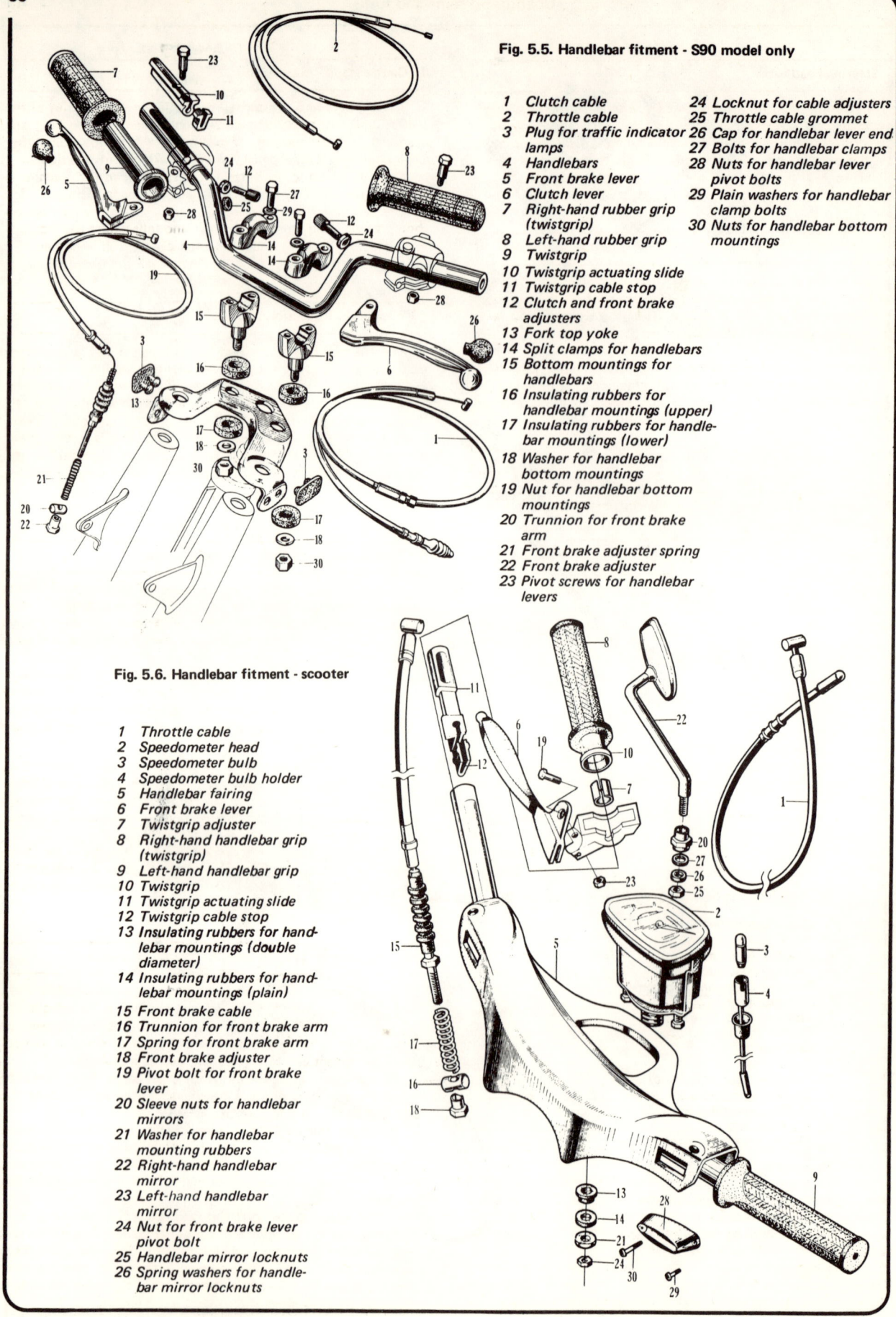

1. Clutch cable
2. Throttle cable
3. Plug for traffic indicator lamps
4. Handlebars
5. Front brake lever
6. Clutch lever
7. Right-hand rubber grip (twistgrip)
8. Left-hand rubber grip
9. Twistgrip
10. Twistgrip actuating slide
11. Twistgrip cable stop
12. Clutch and front brake adjusters
13. Fork top yoke
14. Split clamps for handlebars
15. Bottom mountings for handlebars
16. Insulating rubbers for handlebar mountings (upper)
17. Insulating rubbers for handlebar mountings (lower)
18. Washer for handlebar bottom mountings
19. Nut for handlebar bottom mountings
20. Trunnion for front brake arm
21. Front brake adjuster spring
22. Front brake adjuster
23. Pivot screws for handlebar levers
24. Locknut for cable adjusters
25. Throttle cable grommet
26. Cap for handlebar lever end
27. Bolts for handlebar clamps
28. Nuts for handlebar lever pivot bolts
29. Plain washers for handlebar clamp bolts
30. Nuts for handlebar bottom mountings

Fig. 5.6. Handlebar fitment - scooter

1. Throttle cable
2. Speedometer head
3. Speedometer bulb
4. Speedometer bulb holder
5. Handlebar fairing
6. Front brake lever
7. Twistgrip adjuster
8. Right-hand handlebar grip (twistgrip)
9. Left-hand handlebar grip
10. Twistgrip
11. Twistgrip actuating slide
12. Twistgrip cable stop
13. Insulating rubbers for handlebar mountings (double diameter)
14. Insulating rubbers for handlebar mountings (plain)
15. Front brake cable
16. Trunnion for front brake arm
17. Spring for front brake arm
18. Front brake adjuster
19. Pivot bolt for front brake lever
20. Sleeve nuts for handlebar mirrors
21. Washer for handlebar mounting rubbers
22. Right-hand handlebar mirror
23. Left-hand handlebar mirror
24. Nut for front brake lever pivot bolt
25. Handlebar mirror locknuts
26. Spring washers for handlebar mirror locknuts

Chapter 5/Frame and forks

5 Steering head lock

A steering head lock is attached to the lower fork yoke by two crosshead screws. The tongue of the lock engages with a hole drilled in a plate attached to the steering head column, so that the machine can be left unattended with the handlebars on full left lock. If the lock malfunctions, it must be replaced.

6 Frame assembly - inspection and renovation

1 The frame assembly is unlikely to require attention unless it has been damaged in an accident. Replacement of the complete unit is the only satisfactory course of action when the frame is out of alignment, if only because the special jigs and mandrels essential for resetting the frame will not be available.
2 After a machine has covered an extensive mileage, it is advisable to inspect the frame for signs of cracking or splitting in the vicinity of the engine mounting points. Repairs can be effected by welding.

7 Swinging arm rear fork - dismantling, inspection and reassembly

1 The rear fork of the frame assembly pivots on the rear fork pivot bolt which is carried in rubber bushes. Its action is controlled by two hydraulically-damped rear suspension units that each carry a two-rate compression spring, connected between the swinging arm fork and the frame, one on each side of the machine.
2 To detach the rear fork, remove the rear wheel as described in Chapter 6. Remove the upper and lower halves of the rear chaincase and remove the final drive chain.
3 Unscrew the 10 mm nut attaching each of the rear suspension units to the frame. Remove the domed nut that secures the lower eye of each unit to the swinging arm fork.
4 Unscrew the rear fork pivot nut and withdraw the fork pivot bolt. The swinging arm fork can now be removed from the frame.
5 Check the condition of the rubber bushes in the swinging arm fork pivot. A rubber bonded bush is fitted to each side, which can be pressed out if renewal is necessary. Replace the bushes if they show signs of damage or ageing, or if the pivot bolt is a slack fit. Check also the pivot bolt.
6 Place a straight metal rod across the open ends of the swinging arm fork, where the rear wheel spindle is normally located. Check for twist or deformation. If the amount of twist is more than 1 mm, the swinging arm fork should be replaced. A twisted rear fork will throw the wheels out of track and give the machine poor handling characteristics.
7 To reassemble the swinging arm fork assembly, reverse the procedure detailed above.

8 Rear suspension units - dismantling and inspection

1 The rear suspension units can be partially dismantled to gain access to the springs. Unscrew the upper eye of the unit from the damper rod after slackening the locknut. When the pivot eye has been removed, the top shroud can be pulled off and the spring and spring guide detached. Note the spring is of the two-rate type. If the free length of the spring is below 200 mm, it must be replaced.
2 If the suspension units show signs of leakage or if the damping action is no longer evident, the units should be replaced. The damper unit is sealed and cannot be repaired.

9 Centre stand - inspection

1 The centre stand is attached to the lower extremities of the frame unit, to provide a convenient means of parking the machine on level ground. It pivots on the hollow tube that carries the rear brake pedal, which is retained in position by a split pin. A return spring retracts the stand when the machine is pushed forward, so that it can be wheeled prior to riding.
2 The condition of the return spring and the return action should be checked regularly. If the stand falls whilst the machine is in motion it could catch in some obstacle in the road and unseat the rider.

10 Footrests - inspection and renovation

1 The footrest bar is attached to the bottom of the crankcase of the engine unit by four 8 mm bolts and washers. The bar is malleable and is likely to become bent if the machine is dropped.
2 To straighten the bar first remove it from the machine and detach the footrest rubbers. It can then be bent straight in a vice, using a blow lamp to warm the tube if the bend is severe. Never attempt to straighten the bar whilst it is still attached to the crankcase, otherwise serious damage to the crankcase casting may result.

11 Speedometer - removal and replacement

1 A speedometer of the magnetic type is fitted to these Honda models. It contains also the odometer for recording the total mileage covered by the machine, a small bulb for illuminating the dial during the hours of darkness, and the neutral indicator lamp.
2 The speedometer is held in position by a simple, rear-mounting clamp and two milled nuts, or by a tension spring. To remove the speedometer, unscrew the nuts and withdraw the clamp or release the spring. The speedometer can now be lifted clear, from the top.
3 Although a speedometer on a machine of less than 100 cc capacity is not a statutory requirement in the UK, if one is fitted it must be in good working order. Reference to the mileage reading shown on the odometer is a good way of keeping in pace with the routine maintenance schedules.
4 Apart from defects in the speedometer drive or in the drive cable itself, a speedometer that malfunctions is difficult to repair. Fit a replacement or alternatively entrust the repair to an instrument repair specialist.

12 Speedometer cable - inspection and maintenance

1 It is advisable to detach the speedometer drive cable from time to time, in order to check whether it is adequately lubricated and whether the outer covering is compressed or damaged at any point along its run. A jerky or sluggish speedometer movement can often be attributed to a cable fault.
2 To grease the cable, withdraw the inner cable. After removing the old grease, clean with a petrol soaked rag and examine the cable for broken strands or other damage.
3 Re-grease the cable with high melting point grease, taking care not to grease the last six inches at the point where the cable enters the speedometer head. If this precaution is not observed, grease will work into the speedometer head and immobilise the movement.
4 If the speedometer and the odometer stop working, it is probable that the speedometer cable has broken. Inspection will show whether the inner cable has broken; if so, the inner cable alone can be renewed and reinserted in the outer covering after greasing. Never fit a new inner cable alone if the outer covering is damaged or compressed at any point along its run.

Fig. 5.7. Scooter model frame

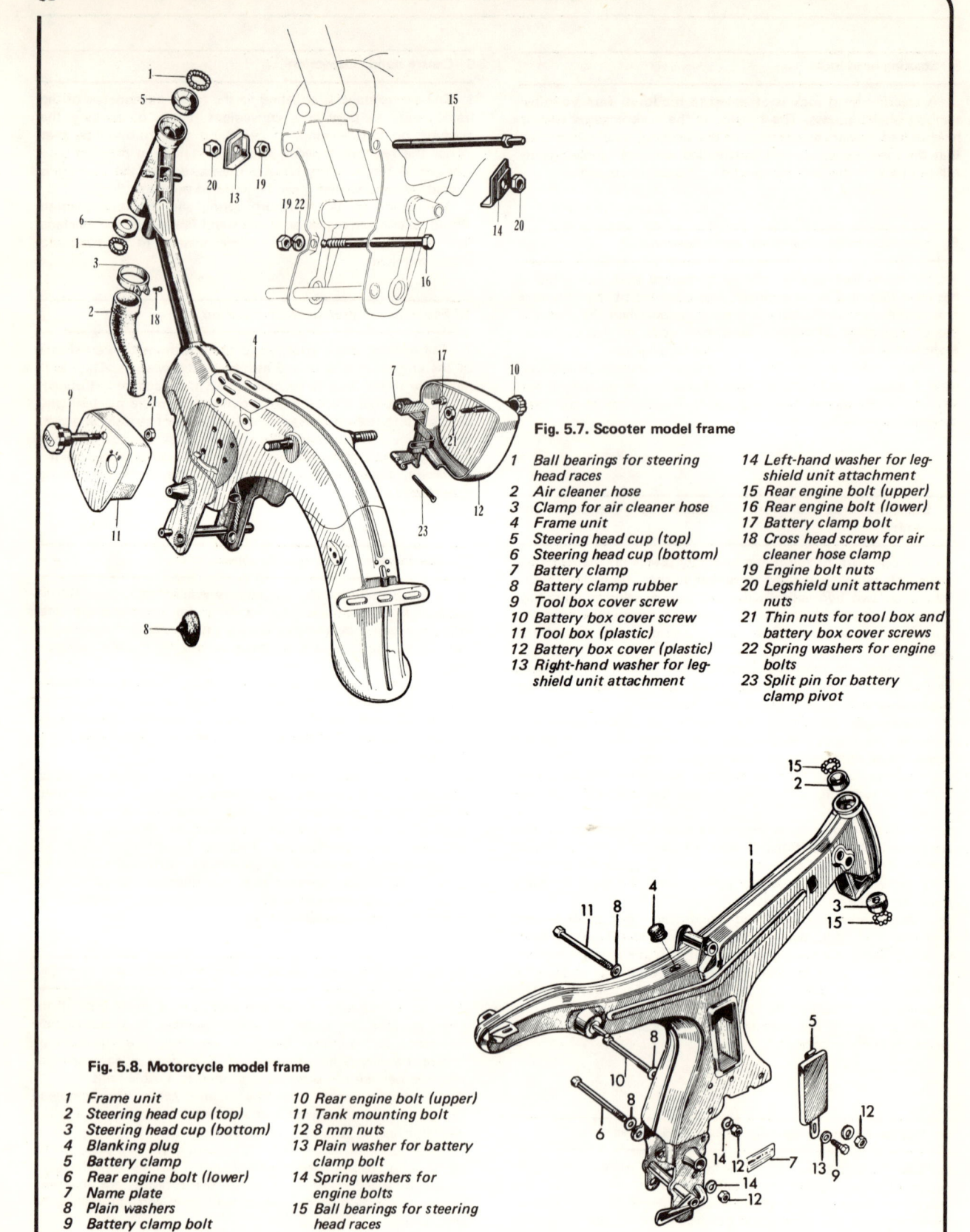

1 Ball bearings for steering head races
2 Air cleaner hose
3 Clamp for air cleaner hose
4 Frame unit
5 Steering head cup (top)
6 Steering head cup (bottom)
7 Battery clamp
8 Battery clamp rubber
9 Tool box cover screw
10 Battery box cover screw
11 Tool box (plastic)
12 Battery box cover (plastic)
13 Right-hand washer for legshield unit attachment
14 Left-hand washer for legshield unit attachment
15 Rear engine bolt (upper)
16 Rear engine bolt (lower)
17 Battery clamp bolt
18 Cross head screw for air cleaner hose clamp
19 Engine bolt nuts
20 Legshield unit attachment nuts
21 Thin nuts for tool box and battery box cover screws
22 Spring washers for engine bolts
23 Split pin for battery clamp pivot

Fig. 5.8. Motorcycle model frame

1 Frame unit
2 Steering head cup (top)
3 Steering head cup (bottom)
4 Blanking plug
5 Battery clamp
6 Rear engine bolt (lower)
7 Name plate
8 Plain washers
9 Battery clamp bolt
10 Rear engine bolt (upper)
11 Tank mounting bolt
12 8 mm nuts
13 Plain washer for battery clamp bolt
14 Spring washers for engine bolts
15 Ball bearings for steering head races

Chapter 5/Frame and fork

13 Speedometer drive gearbox - location and inspection

1 The speedometer drive gearbox is attached to the brake plate of the front brake assembly and is driven internally from the hub. The gearbox rarely gives trouble unless it is not lubricated regularly, in which case the drive may become stiff or part of the drive mechanism shear.

2 The gearbox is retained in position by the front wheel spindle, which passes through the centre. When the spindle is withdrawn, the gearbox will pull free of the brake plate. The drive ring that engages with the revolving hub will be found inside the boss cast in the centre of the front brake plate, from which it can readily be withdrawn. Inspection will show whether the two projecting tongues that take up the drive are broken or damaged.

14 Dualseat - removal

1 The dualseat is removed by detaching the two bolts at the rear of the dualseat that are exposed when the dualseat is raised.

2 The long bolt through the rear carrier can be withdrawn after the dualseat has been detached.

15 Cleaning the plastics mouldings

1 The moulded plastics cycle parts, such as the front mudguard, front fork cover and leg shield cover (scooter models) will not respond to cleaning in the same way as the other metal parts as they are moulded in rigid polyethylene. It is best to wash these parts with a household detergent solution which will remove oil and grease in a most effective manner.

2 Avoid the use of scouring powder as much as possible because this will score the surface of the mouldings and make them more receptive to dirt.

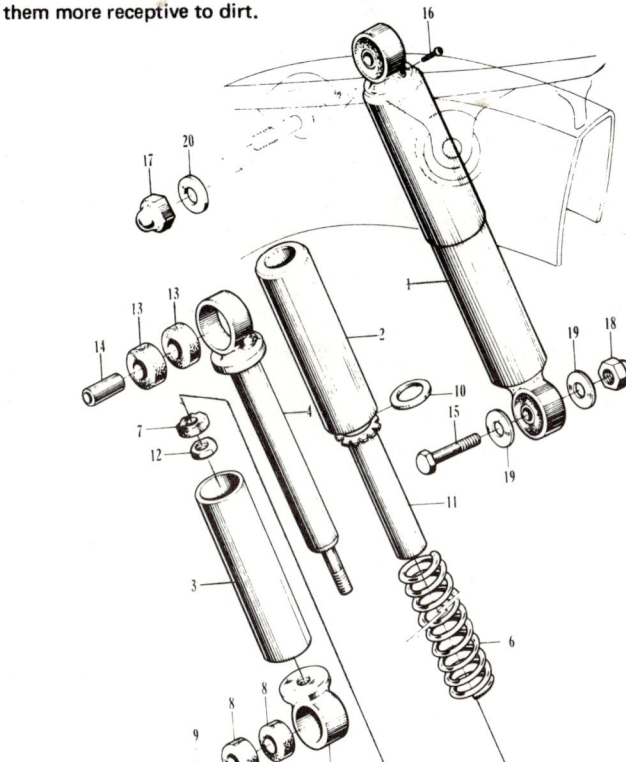

14.1. Removal of rear mount bolts releases dual seat from hinge

16 Cleaning - general

1 After removing all surface dirt with a rag or sponge that is washed frequently in clean water, the application of car polish or wax will give a good finish to the cycle parts of the machine, after they have dried thoroughly. The plated parts should require only a wipe over with a damp rag.

2 If possible, the machine should be wiped over immediately after it has been used in the wet, so that it is not garaged in damp conditions that will promote rusting. Make sure to wipe the chain and if necessary re-oil it, to prevent water from entering the rollers and causing harshness with an accompanying rapid rate of wear. Remember there is little chance of water entering the control cables if they are lubricated regularly, as recommended in the Routine Maintenance section.

Fig. 5.9. Rear suspension units

1 Rear suspension unit complete
2 Upper shroud
3 Lower shroud
4 Sealed damper unit
5 Suspension unit lower pivot
6 Suspension unit spring
7 Rubber stop for suspension unit
8 Rubber bushes for suspension unit lower pivot
9 Bushes for suspension unit lower pivot
10 23 mm washer for spring seating
11 Suspension unit spring guide
12 Locknut for damper rod
13 Rubber bushes for suspension unit upper pivot
14 Bush for suspension unit upper pivot
15 Pivot bolt for suspension unit lower pivot
16 Suspension unit filler screw
17 Domed nut for suspension unit upper pivot stud
18 Domed nut for suspension unit lower pivot bolt
19 Pivot bolt washers (lower)
20 Pivot bolt washers (upper)

16 Fault diagnosis - frame and forks

Symptom	Cause	Remedy
Machine is unduly sensitive to road surface irregularities	Fork and/or rear suspension units damping ineffective	Check oil level in forks. Replace rear suspension units.
Machine rolls at low speeds	Steering head bearings overtight or damaged	Slacken bearing adjustment. If no improvement, dismantle and inspect head bearings.
Machine tends to wander; steering is imprecise	Worn swinging arm suspension bearings	Check and if necessary renew pivot spindle and bush.
Fork action stiff	Fork legs have twisted in yokes or have been drawn together at lower ends	Slacken off spindle nut (clamps), pinch bolts in yokes and fork top nuts. Pump forks several times before retightening from bottom. Add distance pieces to fork spindle (early models).
Forks judder when front brake is applied	Worn fork bushes	Strip forks and replace worn bushes.
	Steering head bearings too slack	Re-adjust to take up play.
Wheels seem out of alignment	Frame distorted as result of accident damage	Check frame after stripping out. If bent, specialist repair is necessary.

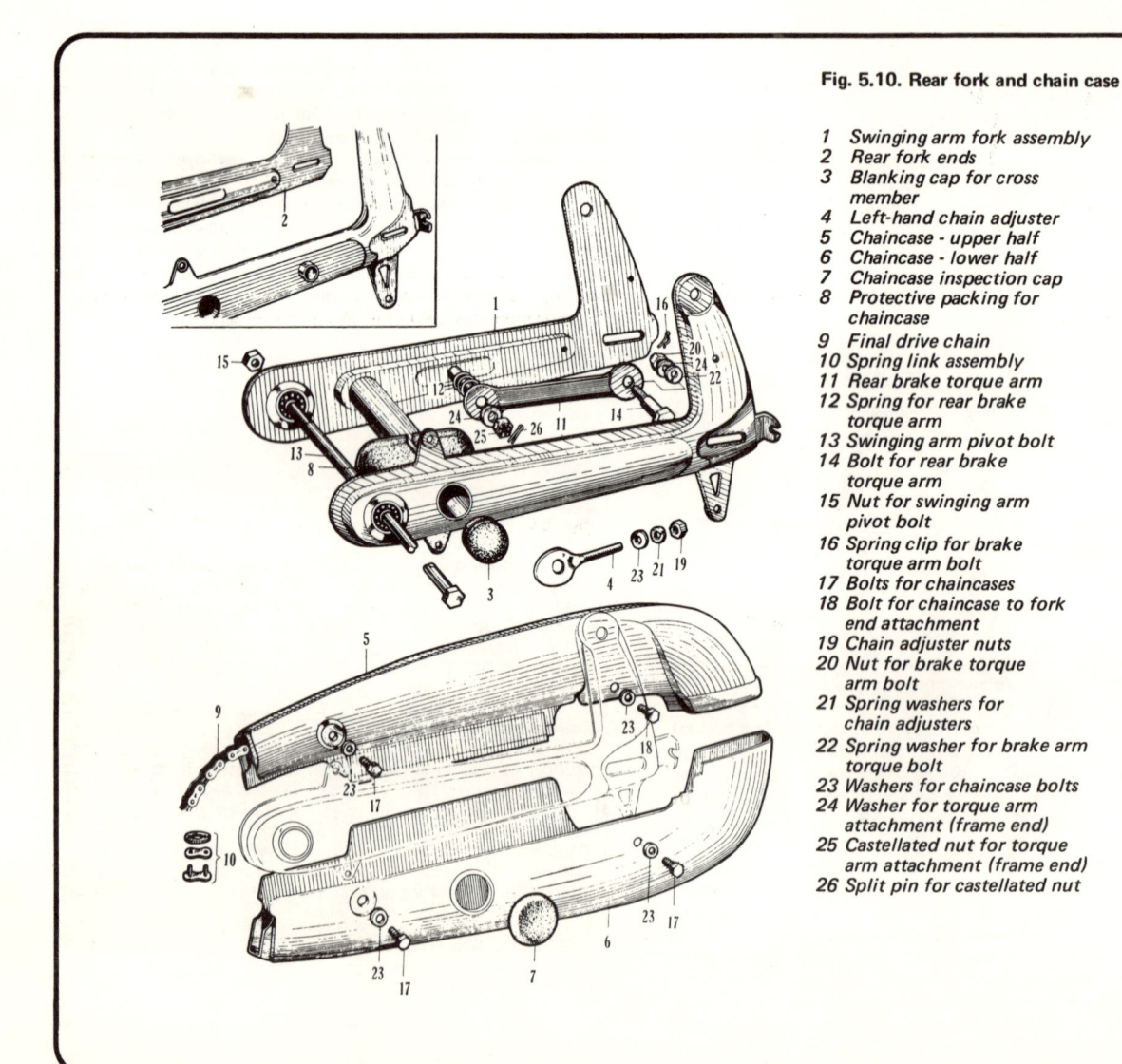

Fig. 5.10. Rear fork and chain case

1 Swinging arm fork assembly
2 Rear fork ends
3 Blanking cap for cross member
4 Left-hand chain adjuster
5 Chaincase - upper half
6 Chaincase - lower half
7 Chaincase inspection cap
8 Protective packing for chaincase
9 Final drive chain
10 Spring link assembly
11 Rear brake torque arm
12 Spring for rear brake torque arm
13 Swinging arm pivot bolt
14 Bolt for rear brake torque arm
15 Nut for swinging arm pivot bolt
16 Spring clip for brake torque arm bolt
17 Bolts for chaincases
18 Bolt for chaincase to fork end attachment
19 Chain adjuster nuts
20 Nut for brake torque arm bolt
21 Spring washers for chain adjusters
22 Spring washer for brake arm torque bolt
23 Washers for chaincase bolts
24 Washer for torque arm attachment (frame end)
25 Castellated nut for torque arm attachment (frame end)
26 Split pin for castellated nut

Chapter 6 Wheels, brakes and final drive

Contents

General description ... 1	Front and rear brakes - adjustment ... 8
Front wheel - inspection and removal ... 2	Cush drive assembly - inspection and renovation ... 9
Front brake assembly - inspection and renovation ... 3	Rear wheel sprocket - removal, inspection and replacement ... 10
Wheel bearings - inspection and replacement ... 4	Final drive chain - inspection ... 11
Front wheel - reassembly and replacement ... 5	Tyres - removal and replacement ... 12
Rear wheel - inspection, removal and renovation ... 6	Fault diagnosis - wheels, brakes and final drive ... 13
Rear brake assembly - inspection, renovation and reassembly ... 7	

Specifications

Wheels	17 inch diameter, front and rear
Tyres	2.25 inch x 17 inch front and rear (S65 and C70 models)
	2.50 inch x 17 inch front and rear (C200, CM90, S90 and C90 models)
Brakes	110 mm diameter, front and rear
Chain size	½ inch x ¼ inch all models

1 General description

Both wheels are of 17 inch diameter and carry tyres of 2.25 inch section (2.50 inch section, 90 cc models), a ribbed tyre at the front and a block tread tyre at the rear. Steel wheel rims are used in conjunction with cast aluminium alloy hubs, each hub containing a 110 mm internal expanding brake. The wheels are not interchangeable because the rear wheel incorporates a special cush drive arrangement to act as a transmission shock absorber. Both wheels are quickly detachable; the rear wheel can be removed from the frame without disturbing the rear wheel sprocket or the final drive chain.

2 Front wheel - inspection and renovation

1 Place the machine on the centre stand so that the front wheel is raised clear of the ground. Spin the wheel and check for rim alignment. Small irregularities can be corrected by tightening the spokes in the affected area, although a certain amount of experience is advisable if over-correction is to be avoided. Any flats in the wheel rim should be evident at the same time. These are more difficult to remove and in most cases the wheel will need to be rebuilt on a new rim. Apart from the effect on stability, there is greater risk of damage to the tyre bead and walls if the machine is run with a deformed wheel.
2 Check for broken or loose spokes. Tapping the spokes is the best guide to tension. A loose spoke will produce a quite different sound and should be tightened by turning the nipple in an anti-clockwise direction. Always re-check for run-out by spinning the wheel again.

2.1. Badly buckled wheel rim

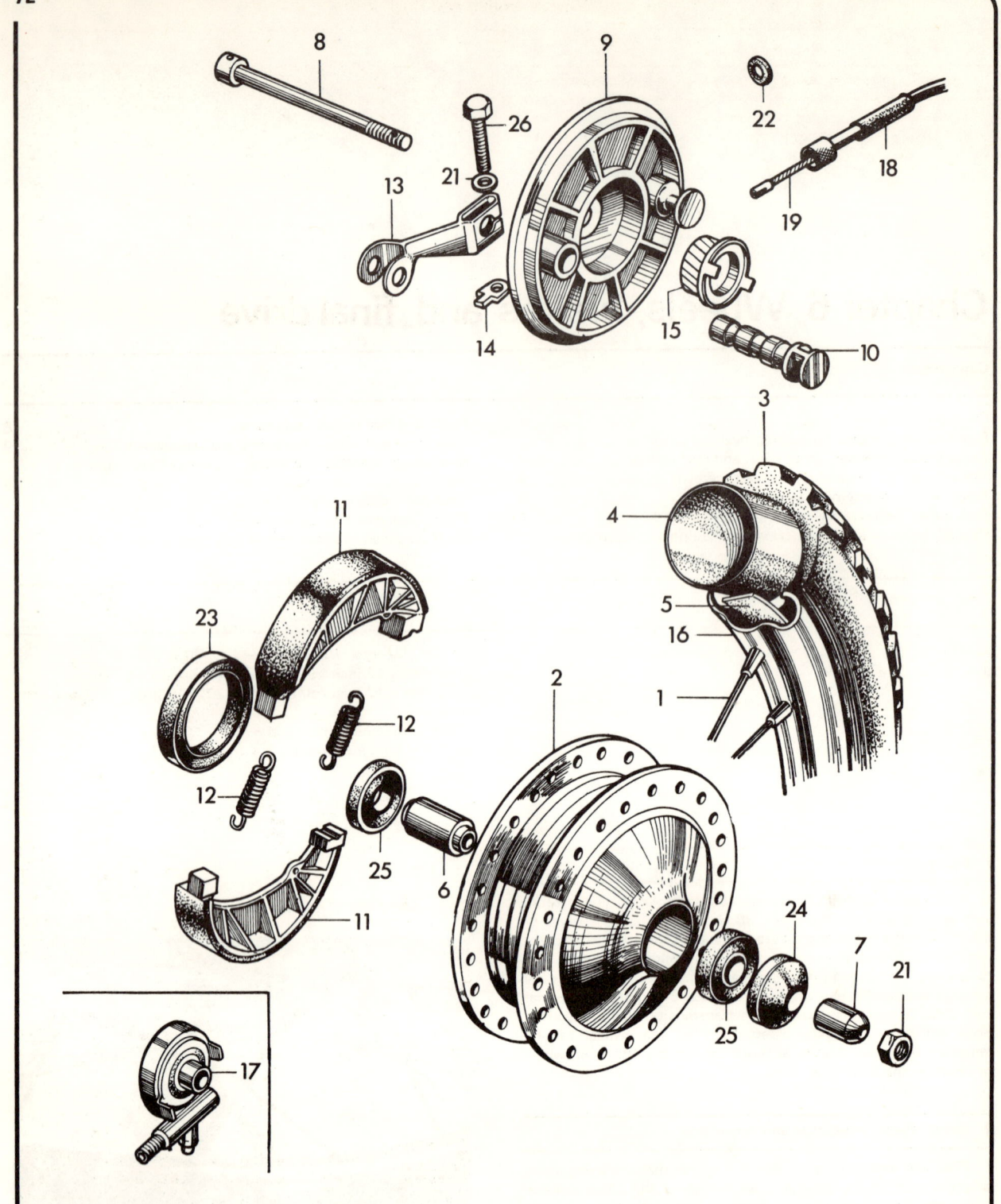

Fig. 6.1. Front wheel and brake

1 Spokes
2 Front wheel hub
3 Front tyre
4 Inner tube
5 Rim tape
6 Front wheel spindle distant piece (within hub)
7 Front wheel spindle
 distance piece
8 Front wheel spindle
9 Front brake plate
10 Brake cam
11 Brake shoes
12 Brake shoe springs
13 Brake operating arm
14 Brake arm clamp nut
15 Speedometer gear
16 Wheel rim
17 Speedometer drive gearbox
18 Speedometer drive cable (outer)
19 Speedometer drive cable (inner)
20 Front wheel spindle nut
21 Brake, arm clamp bolt washer
22 Speedometer pinion washer
23 Front wheel bearing oil seal (right-hand)
24 Front wheel bearing oil seal (left-hand)
25 Front wheel bearings
26 Brake arm clamp bolt

Note: On some models a slightly different design of front brake plate may be fitted, depending on the method of anchoring the brake plate

Chapter 6/Wheels, brakes and final drive

3 Front brake assembly - inspection, renovation and reassembly

1 The front brake assembly complete with brake plate can be withdrawn from the front wheel hub after the wheel spindle has been pulled out and the wheel removed from the forks. Refer to Chapter 5.2, commencing with section 7.
2 Examine the condition of the brake linings. If they are wearing thin or unevenly the brake shoes should be replaced.
3 To remove the brake shoes from the brake plate, pull them apart whilst lifting them upwards in the form of a 'V'. When they are clear of the brake plate, the return springs can be removed and the shoes separated. Note that the speedometer drive gear may fall clear of the brake plate during this operation. It is no longer held captive when the brake plate is removed from the hub.
4 Before replacing the brake shoes, check that the brake operating cam is working smoothly and not binding in its pivot. The cam can be removed for greasing by slackening the pinch bolt on the cable operating arm and withdrawing the arm, after first marking its position on the splines to aid correct relocation.
5 Check also the inner surface of the brake drum, on which the brake shoes bear. The surface should be smooth and free from score marks or indentations, otherwise reduced braking efficiency is inevitable. Remove all traces of brake lining dust and wipe with a rag dipped in petrol to remove any traces of grease or oil.
6 To reassemble the brake shoes on the brake plate, fit the return springs and force the shoes apart, holding them in a 'V' formation. If they are now located with the brake operating cam and pivot they can usually be snapped into position by pressing downwards. Do not use excessive force, otherwise the shoes may be distorted permanently.

4 Wheel bearings - inspection and replacement

1 Access to the wheel bearings is gained when the brake plate has been removed from the front wheel. There is an oil seal in front of the bearing on the brake drum side, to prevent grease from reaching the brake operating parts. This seal should be prised out of position and a new replacement obtained.
2 The wheel bearings, of the ball journal type, are a drive fit in the hub. Use a double diameter drift to displace the bearings from the hub, working from each side of the hub. When the first bearing emerges from the hub the hollow distance collar that separates them can be removed.
3 Remove all the old grease from the hub and bearings, giving the latter a final wash in petrol. Check the bearings for play or signs of roughness when they are turned. If there is any doubt about their condition, replace them.
4 Before replacing the bearings, first pack the hub with new grease. Then grease both bearings and drive them back into position with the same double diameter drift, not forgetting the distance collar that separates them. Fit the replacement oil seals in front of the bearing on the brake drum side.

5 Front wheel - reassembly and replacement

1 Place the front brake plate and brake assembly in the brake drum and align the front wheel with the forks. Insert the front wheel spindle and replace the spindle washer, nut and split pin. Note that it will be necessary also to reconnect the brake torque arm to the front brake plate and replace the split pin, before the front wheel spindle is tightened, where this type of anchorage is used.
2 Reconnect the speedometer drive cable and the front brake cable. Check that the front brake functions correctly, particularly if the brake operating arm has been removed and replaced, during the dismantling operation.

3.1. Brake assembly is free when spindle is withdrawn

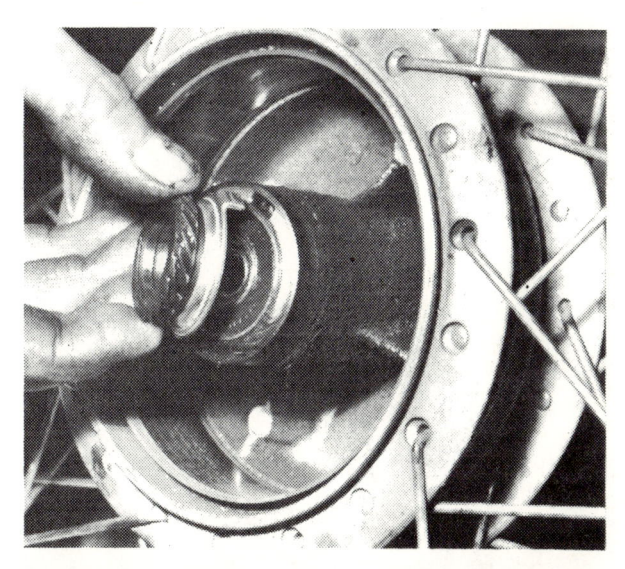

3.3. Speedometer drive gear tongues engage with slots in hub

3.6. Snap brake shoes back into position as shown

Fig. 6.2. Rear wheel and brake

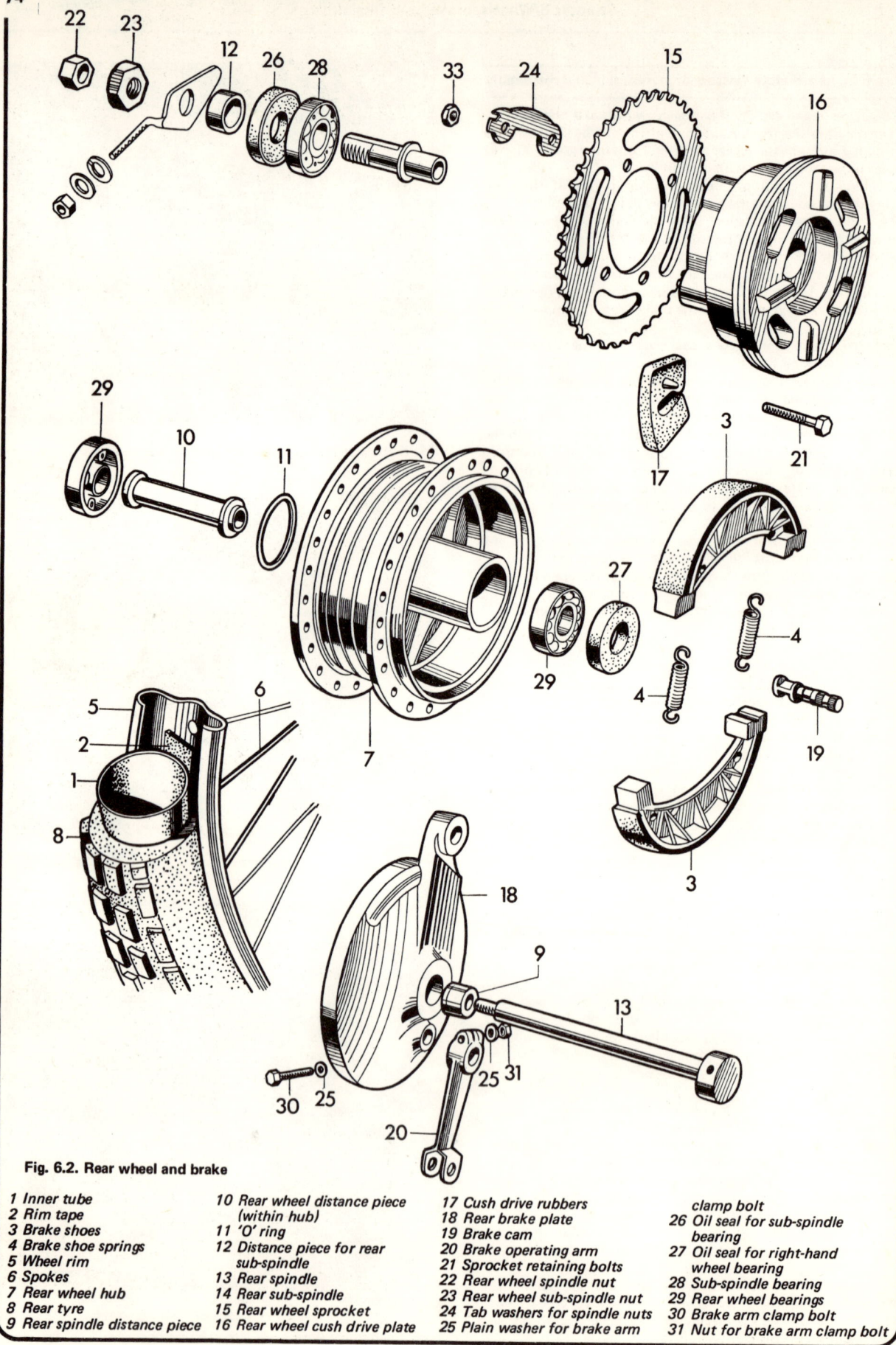

1 Inner tube
2 Rim tape
3 Brake shoes
4 Brake shoe springs
5 Wheel rim
6 Spokes
7 Rear wheel hub
8 Rear tyre
9 Rear spindle distance piece
10 Rear wheel distance piece (within hub)
11 'O' ring
12 Distance piece for rear sub-spindle
13 Rear spindle
14 Rear sub-spindle
15 Rear wheel sprocket
16 Rear wheel cush drive plate
17 Cush drive rubbers
18 Rear brake plate
19 Brake cam
20 Brake operating arm
21 Sprocket retaining bolts
22 Rear wheel spindle nut
23 Rear wheel sub-spindle nut
24 Tab washers for spindle nuts
25 Plain washer for brake arm clamp bolt
26 Oil seal for sub-spindle bearing
27 Oil seal for right-hand wheel bearing
28 Sub-spindle bearing
29 Rear wheel bearings
30 Brake arm clamp bolt
31 Nut for brake arm clamp bolt

5.1. Do not forget to tighten brake anchorage bolt

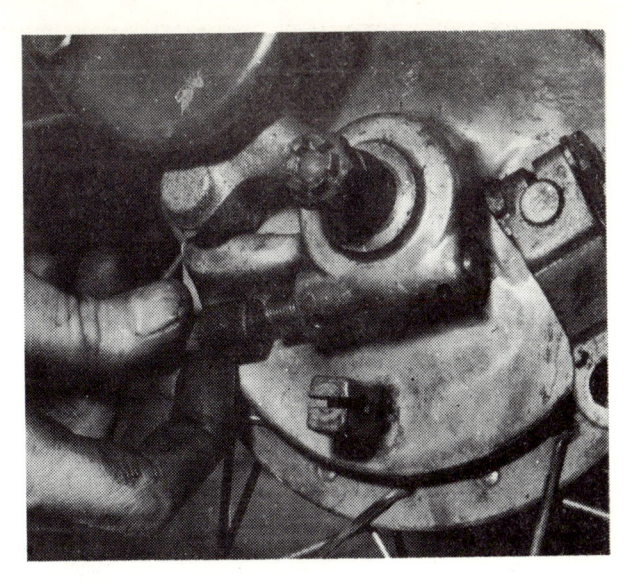

5.2. Speedometer drive cable has screw-on connector

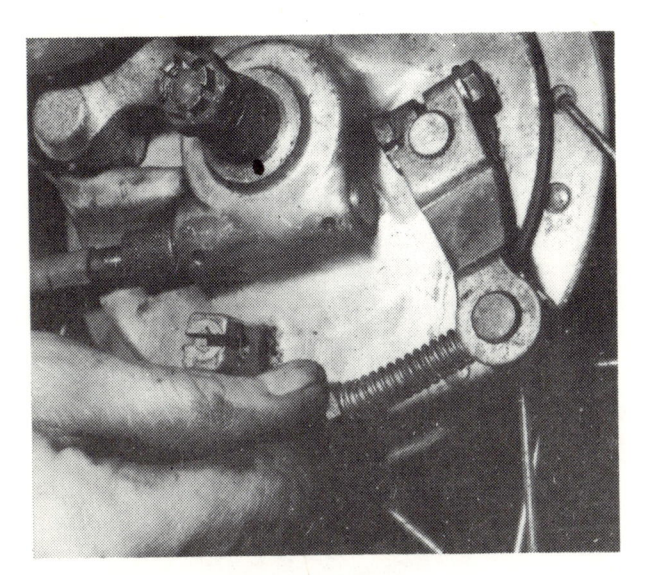

5.2A. Engage cable end with operating lever first

5.2B. Pull on cable and slide outer cover in cable stop

6 Rear wheel - inspection, removal and renovation

1 Before attempting to remove the rear wheel, check for rim alignment, damage to the rim and loose or broken spokes by following the procedure relating to the front wheel, in the preceding section.

2 To remove the rear wheel, place the machine on the centre stand so that the wheel is raised clear of the ground. Remove the silencer (all models with a downswept system only). Remove also the brake adjusting nut and separate the brake rod from the operating arm of the rear brake. Slacken and remove the nut and bolt from the rear brake torque arm, at the brake plate anchorage.

3 Remove the centre of the two rear wheel spindle nuts and pull the spindle from the hub. Remove the distance pieces if they have not fallen clear and disengage the hub from the cush drive assembly by pulling the wheel towards the right-hand side of the machine. The wheel can now be removed from the frame complete with the rear brake assembly, leaving the rear sprocket and final drive chain in position.

4 The rear brake assembly can be removed and dismantled by following the procedure given for the front brake, in section 3 of this Chapter. The brake assemblies differ only with regard to the design of the brake plate.

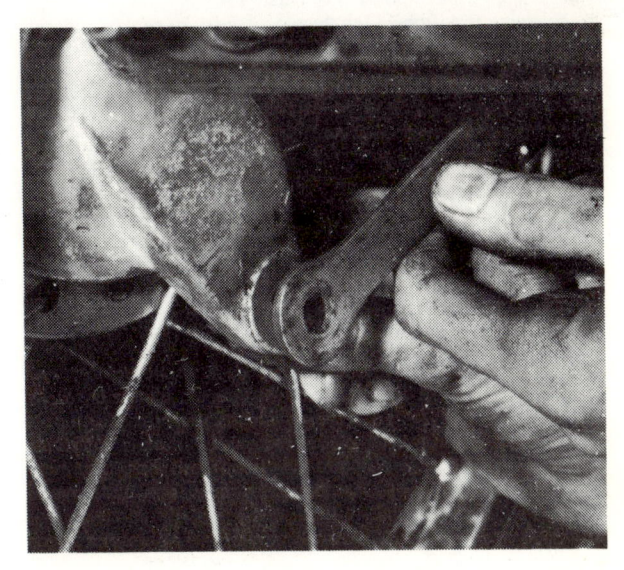

6.2. Detach torque arm connection at brake plate

5 The rear wheel bearings, of the ball journal type, are a drive fit in the hub. The same double diameter drift used for the front wheel bearings can be used to displace them, even though the front and rear wheel bearings are not interchangeable. The two bearings are separated by a hollow distance collar which can be removed when the first bearing is displaced from the hub.

6 Repack the hub and bearings with grease before reassembly, as detailed in section 4 of this Chapter. Note that there is an oil seal in front of the right-hand bearing (brake drum side) to prevent grease from reaching the brake assembly.

7 Rear brake assembly - inspection, renovation and reassembly

1 The rear brake assembly complete with brake plate can be withdrawn from the rear wheel hub after the wheel spindle has been pulled out and the wheel removed from the rear forks. Refer to the preceding section of this Chapter.

2 Follow an identical procedure to that relating to the front brake, as given in section 3 of this Chapter. The brake assemblies are identical, apart from differences in the design of the brake plates.

8 Front and rear brakes - adjustment

1 The amount of free play in both brake assemblies should be 2 - 3 cm before the brake begins to bite. The amount of free play is measured at the handlebar lever in the case of the front brake and at the foot pedal in the case of the rear brake. Adjustment is effected by turning the adjusting nut close to the operating arm, in each case.

2 Check that the brakes pull off correctly when the lever and pedal are released. Sluggish action can usually be traced to a broken return spring on the brake shoes or a tendency for the operating cam to bind in its bush.

9 Cush drive assembly - inspection and renovation

1 The cush drive assembly is contained in the left-hand side of the rear wheel hub. It comprises a set of rubber buffers housed within a series of vanes cast in the hub shell. A plate attached to the final drive sprocket has four cast-in dogs that engage with slots in these rubbers when the wheel is replaced in the frame. The drive is transmitted to the rear wheel via these rubbers, which absorb any surges or roughness in the drive which may otherwise give the impression of harshness.

2 Examine the rubbers for signs of damage or general deterioration. Replace the rubbers if there is any doubt about their condition.

10 Rear wheel sprocket - removal, inspection and replacement

1 The rear wheel sprocket can be removed as a separate unit after the rear wheel has been detached from the frame as described in section 6 of this Chapter. Alternatively, it can be removed with the rear wheel complete if both halves of the rear chaincase are removed (top run only, some S90 models) and the final drive chain is detached by removing the larger of the two rear wheel spindle nuts.

2 Check the condition of the sprocket teeth. If they are hooked, chipped or badly worn, the sprocket should be replaced. It is attached to the cush drive plate by four bolts with tab washers.

3 It is bad practice to renew one sprocket on its own. The final drive sprockets should always be renewed as a pair and a new chain fitted, otherwise rapid wear will call for an even earlier replacement on the next occasion.

4 An additional bearing is housed within the cush drive plate, in the centre of the sprocket. This bearing of the journal ball type, should be pulled off the rear spindle sleeve whilst the cush

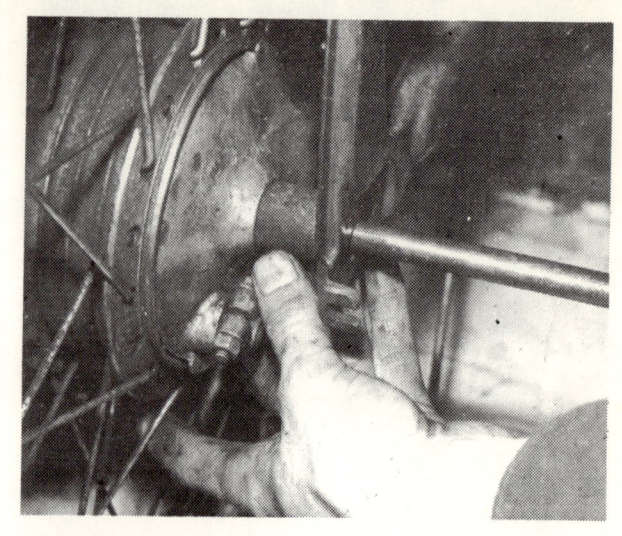

6.3. Make sure distance piece is not misplaced when spindle is withdrawn

6.5. Bearing is exposed after oil seal is removed

6.5A. Use drift of correct size for removing and replacing bearings

6.5B. Use care when fitting new oil seal to avoid damage

10.1. Rear wheel cush drive assembly

10.1A. Large outer nut retains sprocket assembly

10.4. Detachable stub spindle

10.4A. Stub spindle has bearing within cush drive centre

10.4B. Bearing has own oil seal

drive assembly is separated, washed out and repacked with new grease. Replace, if the bearing has any play or if it shows signs of roughness. An oil seal in front of this bearing excludes road grit and water.

5 The rear wheel assembly is refitted to the frame by reversing the dismantling procedure given in this section. Make quite sure that the rear brake torque arm is replaced correctly, the nut and bolt fully tightened and the split pin replaced. If the torque arm works loose, the brake plate will revolve when the rear brake is applied and lock the rear wheel a situation that can lead to a skid and the possibility of an accident. Check also that the rear brake functions correctly, particularly if the operating arm has been removed and replaced.

11 Final drive, chain - inspection

1 The final drive chain is fully enclosed within a chaincase except in the case of some S90 models where it is protected by a chainguard over the top run only. Periodically, the tension of the chain will need to be adjusted, to compensate for wear. This is accomplished by sliding the rear wheel backwards in the ends of the rear fork, using the drawbolt adjusters provided. The rear wheel spindle nuts must be slackened before the drawbolts can be turned; also the torque arm bolt on the rear brake plate.

2 The chain is in correct adjustment if there is from 1 - 2 cm free play in the middle of the lower run. An inspection plug in the lower section of the full chaincase permits access to the chain to check whether the tension is correct.

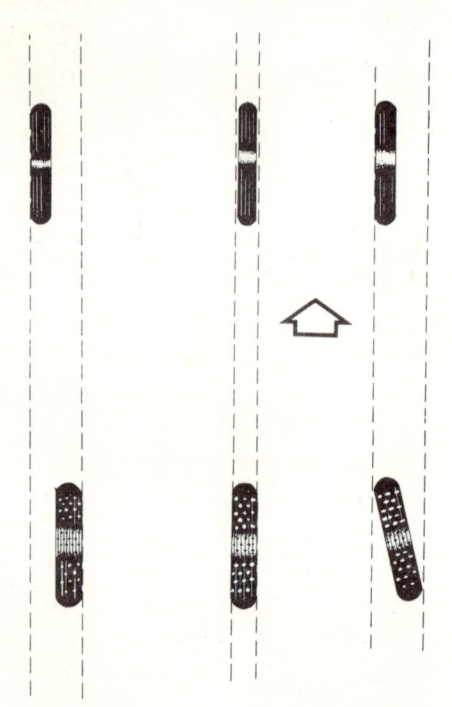

Fig. 6.3. Method of checking wheel alignment

10.5. Do not forget to replace the plastics strip

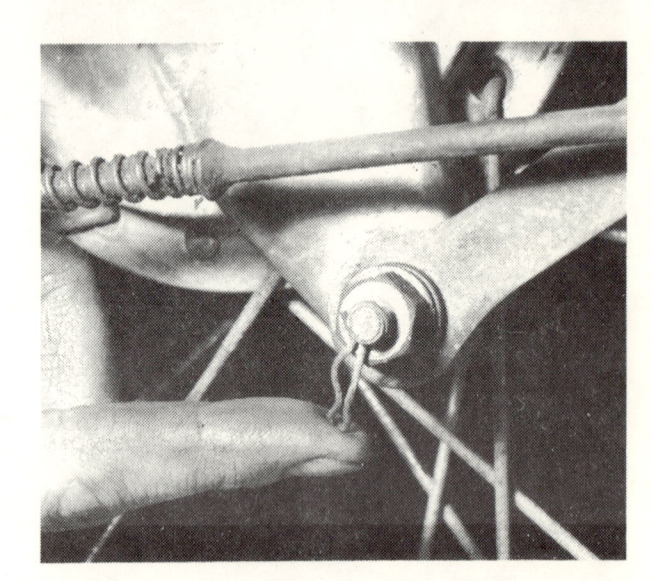

10.5A. Always fit spring clip to lock torque arm bolt

11.2. Check for correct chain tension in middle of bottom run

Chapter 6/Wheels, brakes and final drive

3 Always adjust the drawbolts an identical amount, otherwise the rear wheel will be thrown out of alignment. Later models have centre punch marks to make this adjustment easier. Wheel alignment can be checked by running a plank of wood parallel to the machine, so that it touches the wheel rims. If wheel alignment is correct, the plank will touch both sides of the wheel rim of both wheels, as illustrated in the accompanying diagram.

4 After a period of running, the chain will require lubrication. Lack of oil will accelerate wear of both chain and sprockets and lead to harsh transmission. The chain fitted to the sports models will require more frequent attention because it is more exposed. The application of engine oil from an oil can will serve as satisfactory lubricant, but it is preferable to remove the chain and immerse it in a molten lubricant such as "Linklyfe", after it has been cleaned in a paraffin bath. This latter type of lubricant achieves better penetration of the chain links and rollers and is less likely to be thrown off when the chain is in motion.

5 To check whether the chain requires replacement, lay it endwise in a straight line and compress it so that all play is taken up. Anchor one end and then pull on the other end to take up the end play in the other direction. If the chain extends by more than the distance between two adjacent rollers, it should be replaced in conjunction with the two sprockets. Note that this check should be made after the chain has been washed but before any lubricant is applied, otherwise the lubricant will take up some of the play.

6 When replacing the chain, make sure the spring link is correctly seated, with the closed end facing the direction of travel.

Tyre fitting appears overleaf and fault diagnosis on page 82

11.3. Frame has graduation marks to aid alignment of both adjusters

11.6. Use rear wheel sprocket to make fitting of spring link easy

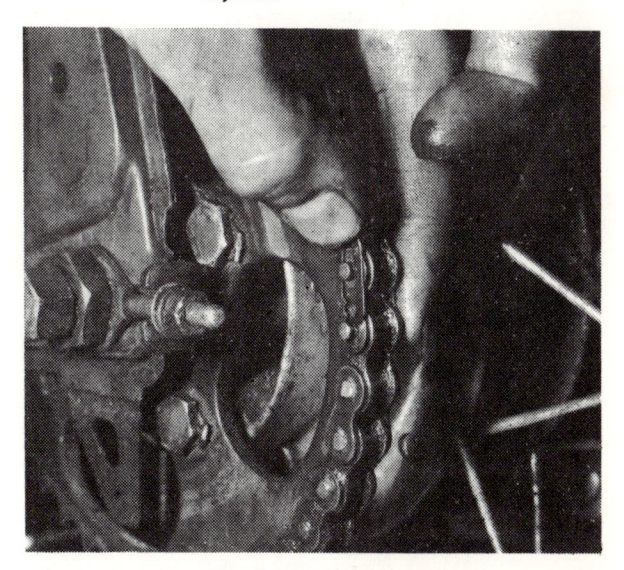

11.6A. Fit spring link with closed end facing direction of chain travel

12 Tyres - removal and replacement

1 At some time or other the need will arise to remove and replace the tyres, either as the result of a puncture or because a replacement is required to offset wear. To the inexperienced, tyre changing represents a formidable task yet if a few simple rules are observed and the technique learned, the whole operation is surprisingly simple.

2 To remove the tyre from either wheel, first detach the wheel from the machine by following the procedure in Chapters 5.2 or 6.6, depending on whether the front or the rear wheel is involved. Deflate the tyre by removing the valve insert and when it is fully deflated, push the bead of the tyre away from the wheel rim on both sides so that the bead enters the centre well of the rim. Remove the locking cap and push the tyre valve into the tyre itself.

3 Insert a tyre lever close to the valve and lever the edge of the tyre over the outside of the wheel rim. Very little force should be necessary; if resistance is encountered it is probably due to the fact that the tyre beads have not entered the well of the wheel rim all the way round the tyre.

4 Once the tyre has been edged over the wheel rim it is easy to work around the wheel rim so that the tyre is completely free on one side. At this stage, the inner tube can be removed.

5 Working from the other side of the wheel, ease the other edge of the tyre over the outside of the wheel rim that is furthest away. Continue to work around the rim until the tyre is free completely from the rim.

6 If a puncture has necessitated the removal of the tyre, re-inflate the inner tube and immerse it in a bowl of water to trace the source of the leak. Mark its position and deflate the tube. Dry the tube and clean the area around the puncture with a petrol-soaked rag. When the surface has dried, apply the rubber solution and allow this to dry before removing the backing from the patch and applying the patch to the surface.

7 It is best to use a patch of the self-vulcanising type, which will form a very permanent repair. Note that it may be necessary to remove a protective covering from the top surface of the patch after it has sealed in position. Inner tubes made from synthetic rubber may require a special type of patch and adhesive, if a satisfactory bond is to be achieved.

8 Before replacing the tyre, check the inside to make sure the agent that caused the puncture is not trapped. Check also the outside of the tyre, particularly the tread area, to make sure nothing is trapped that may cause a further puncture.

9 If the inner tube has been patched on a number of past occasions, or if there is a tear or large hole, it is preferable to discard it and fit a replacement. Sudden deflation may cause an accident, particularly if it occurs with the front wheel.

10 To replace the tyre, inflate the inner tube sufficiently for it to assume a circular shape but only just. Then push it into the tyre so that it is enclosed completely. Lay the tyre on the wheel at an angle and insert the valve through the rim tape and the hole in the wheel rim. Attach the locking cap on the first few threads, sufficient to hold the valve captive in its correct location.

11 Starting at the point furthest from the valve, push the tyre bead over the edge of the wheel rim until it is located in the central well. Continue to work around the tyre in this fashion until the whole of one side of the tyre is on the rim. It may be necessary to use a tyre lever during the final stages.

12 Make sure there is no pull on the tyre valve and again commencing with the area furthest from the valve, ease the other bead of the tyre over the edge of the rim. Finish with the area close to the valve, pushing the valve up into the tyre until the locking cap touches the rim. This will ensure the inner tube is not trapped when the last section of the bead is edged over the rim with a tyre lever.

13 Check that the inner tube is not trapped at any point. Re-inflate the inner tube, and check that the tyre is seating correctly around the wheel rim. There should be a thin rib moulded around the wall of the tyre on both sides, which should be equidistant from the wheel rim at all points. If the tyre is unevenly located on the rim, try bouncing the wheel when the tyre is at the recommended pressure. It is probable that one of the beads has not pulled clear of the centre well.

14 Always run the tyres at the recommended pressures and never under or over-inflate. The correct pressures for solo use are given in the specifications section of this Chapter. If a pillion passenger is carried, increase the rear tyre pressure only.

15 Tyre replacement is aided by dusting the side walls, particularly in the vicinity of the beads, with a liberal coating of french chalk. Washing-up liquid can also be used to good effect, but this has the disadvantage of causing the inner surfaces of the wheel rim to rust.

16 Never replace the inner tube and tyre without the rim tape in position. If this precaution is overlooked there is good chance of the ends of the spoke nipples chafing the inner tube and causing a crop of punctures.

17 Never fit a tyre that has a damaged tread of side walls. Apart from the legal aspects, there is a very great risk of a blow-out, which can have serious consequences on any two-wheel vehicle.

18 Tyre valves rarely give trouble, but it is always advisable to check whether the valve itself is leaking before removing the tyre. Do not forget to fit the dust cap, which forms an effective second seal.

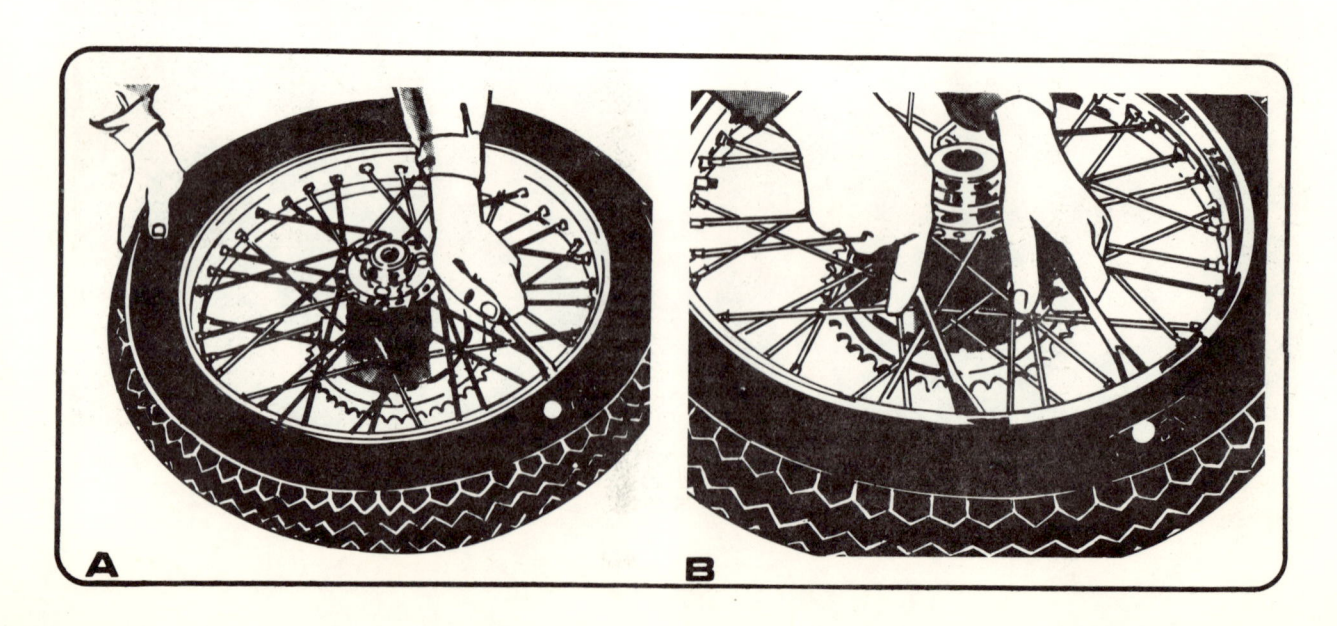

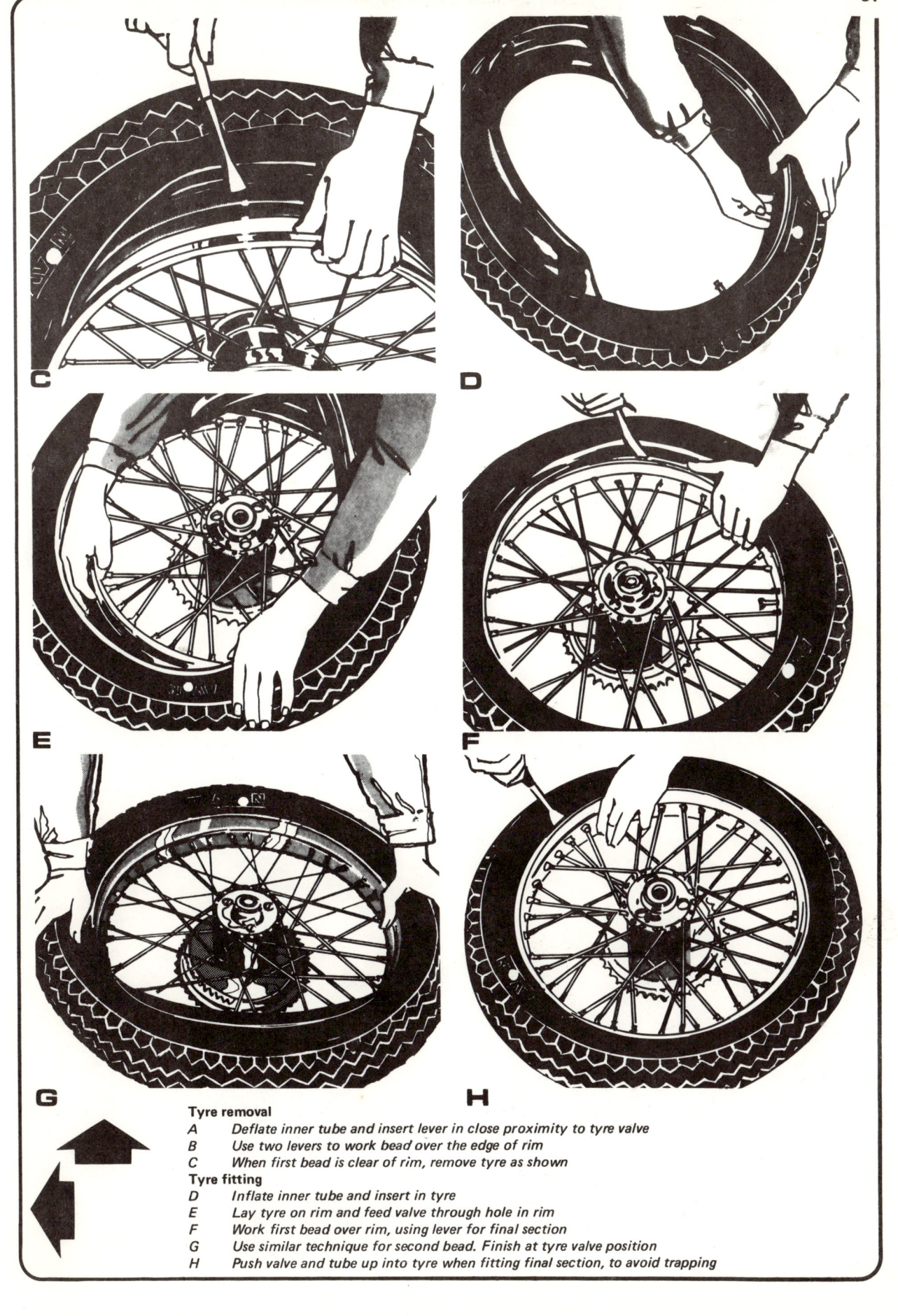

Tyre removal
- A   Deflate inner tube and insert lever in close proximity to tyre valve
- B   Use two levers to work bead over the edge of rim
- C   When first bead is clear of rim, remove tyre as shown

Tyre fitting
- D   Inflate inner tube and insert in tyre
- E   Lay tyre on rim and feed valve through hole in rim
- F   Work first bead over rim, using lever for final section
- G   Use similar technique for second bead. Finish at tyre valve position
- H   Push valve and tube up into tyre when fitting final section, to avoid trapping

13 Fault diagnosis - wheels, brakes and final drive

Symptom	Cause	Remedy
Handlebars oscillate at low speeds	Buckle or flat in wheel rim, most probably front wheel	Check rim alignment by spinning wheel. Correct by retensioning spokes or by having wheel rebuilt on new rim.
	Tyre not straight on rim	Check tyre alignment.
Machine lacks power and accelerates poorly	Brakes binding	Warm brake drums provide best evidence. Re-adjust brakes.
Brakes grab when applied gently	Ends of brake shoes not chamfered	Chamfer with file.
	Elliptical brake drum	Lightly skim in lathe (specialist attention needed).
Brake pull-off sluggish	Brake cam binding in housing	Free and grease.
	Weak brake shoe springs	Replace if springs not displaced.
Harsh transmission	Worn or badly adjusted chains	Adjust or replace as necessary.
	Hooked or badly worn sprockets	Replace as a pair.

Chapter 7 Electrical system

Contents

General description ... 1	Flashing indicators - replacement of bulbs ... 9
Flywheel generators - checking output ... 2	Flasher unit - location and replacement ... 10
Battery - inspection and maintenance ... 3	Neutral indicator bulb - replacement ... 11
Battery - charging procedure ... 4	Speedometer bulb - replacement ... 12
Selenium rectifier - general description ... 5	Horn - location and adjustment.. ... 13
Fuse - location and replacement ... 6	Ignition and lighting switch ... 14
Headlamp - replacing bulbs and adjusting beam height ... 7	Wiring - layout and inspection ... 15
Stop and tail lamp - replacing bulbs ... 8	

Specifications

Battery (lead acid, 6 volt)
- Type ... Yuasa G2H, MBC, B37–6A, MA36A or B36–6 depending on model
- Capacity ... 2, 4, 5.5 or 6 amp hours depending on model
- Earth lead ... Negative

Fuse unit ...
- 7 amp (S65)
- 10 amp (S90, CM90)
- 15 amp (C90)

Lighting
- Headlamp ... 25/25W (all models except S65 and C70)
- 15/15W (S65 and C70)
- Tail/stop ... 2/6W All models
- Flashing indicators ... 8W All models
- Neutral indicator ... 1.5W All models
- Speedometer bulb ... 1.5W All models

1 General description

Two types of 6 volt electrical system are fitted to the Honda models, depending on the specification of the model. The 65 cc - 90 cc C200, CM90, C90, S90 and S70 models have a flywheel a.c. generator of the rotating magnet type which gives a high output. The S65 model has a flywheel magneto generator that supplies the ignition system without dependence on the battery. Both systems contain provision for charging the battery and supplying the lighting and other electrical loads after converting the output to d.c. by means of a rectifier.

2 Flywheel generators - checking output

As explained in Chapter 4.2, the output from either type of generator can be checked only with specialised test equipment of the multi-meter type. If the generator is suspect, it should be checked by either a Honda agent or an auto-electrical expert.

3 Battery - inspection and maintenance

1 Two types of Yuasa battery having different amp-hour capacities are fitted to the Honda 65 cc - 90 cc models. Most models use the 6 amp-hour battery, with the exception of the S65 which has only a 2 amp-hour battery.

2 The transparent case of the battery allows the upper and lower levels of the electrolyte to be observed without need to remove the battery. Batteries of the lead/acid type are employed. Maintenance is normally limited to keeping the electrolyte level within the prescribed upper and lower limits and making sure that the vent tube is not blocked. The lead plates and their separators can also be seen through the transparent case, a further guide to the condition of the battery.

3 Unless acid is spilt, as may occur when the machine falls over, the electrolyte should always be topped up with distilled water, to restore the correct level. If acid is spilt on any part of the machine, it should be neutralised with an alkali such as washing soda and washed away with plenty of water, otherwise serious

corrosion will occur. Top up with sulphuric acid of the correct specific gravity (1.260 - 1.280) only when spillage has occurred.
4 It is seldom practicable to repair a cracked case because the acid in the joint prevents the formation of an effective seal. It is always best to replace a cracked battery, especially in view of the corrosion that will be caused by the leakage of acid.
5 Never check the condition of a battery by shorting the terminals. The very heavy current flow resulting from this sudden discharge will cause the battery to overheat, with consequent damage to the plates and the compound they hold.
6 If the machine is laid up for any time, it is advisable to disconnect and remove the battery. It should not be allowed to discharge completely, otherwise sulphation is liable to occur, an irreversible change in the condition of the plates that will render the battery useless.

4 Battery - charging procedure

1 Whilst the machine is running it is unlikely that the battery will require attention other than routine maintenance because the generator will keep it charged. However, if the machine is used for a succession of short journeys mainly during the hours of darkness when the lights are in full use, it is unlikely that the output from the generator will be able to keep pace with the heavy electrical demand. Under these circumatances it will be necessary to remove the battery from time to time, to have it recharged independently.
2 The normal charging rate for the two types of battery fitted to the Honda 65 cc - 90 cc models is 0.2 amps. A more rapid charge can be given in an emergency, in which case the charging rate can be raised to 0.6 - 1.0 amps. The higher charge rate should be avoided if possible because this will eventually shorten the working life of the battery.
3 When the battery has been removed from a machine that has been laid up, a 'refresher' charge should be given every six weeks if the battery is to be maintained in good condition.

5 Selenium rectifier - general description

1 The function of the selenium rectifier is to convert the a.c. produced by the generator to d.c. so that it can be used to charge the battery and operate the lighting circuit etc. All models employ a full-wave rectifier; with the exception of the S65 model, which has a half-wave rectifier.
2 The rectifier is located in a position where it is not exposed to water or battery acid, which will cause it to malfunction. The question of access is of relatively little importance because the rectifier is unlikely to give trouble during normal service. It is not practicable to repair a damaged rectifier; replacement is the only satisfactory solution.
3 Damage to the rectifier is likely to occur, however, if the machine is run without the battery for any period of time. A high voltage will develop in the absence of any load on the coil, which will cause a reverse flow of current and consequent damage to the rectifier cells.
4 It is not possible to check whether the rectifier is functioning correctly without the appropriate test equipment. A Honda agent or an auto-electrical expert are best qualified to advise in such cases.
5 Do not loosen the rectifier locking nut (painted) or bend, cut, scratch or rotate the selenium wafers. Any such action will cause the electrode alloy coating to peel and destroy the working action.

6 Fuse - location and replacement

1 A fuse is incorporated in the electrical system to give protection from a sudden overload, such as may occur during a short circuit. The fuse is located within the fuse holder attached to the positive lead of the battery. All models have either a 10 amp or a 14 amp fuse, (see wiring diagrams) with the exception of the S65 model (7 amps).

2 If a fuse blows it should be replaced, after checking to ensure that no obvious short circuit has occurred. If the second fuse blows shortly afterwards, the electrical circuit should be checked in order to trace the fault.
3 When a fuse blows whilst running the machine and no spare is available, a 'get you home' dodge is to remove the blown fuse and wrap it in silver paper before replacing it in the fuse holder. The silver paper will restore the electrical continuity by bridging the broken fuse wire. This expedient should never be used if there is evidence of a short circuit, otherwise more serious damage will be caused. Replace the blown fuse at the earliest possible opportunity, to restore the full circuit protection.

7 Headlamp - replacing bulbs and adjusting beam height

1 To remove the headlamp rim, unscrew the crosshead screw at the bottom of the rim. The reflector unit is captive with the rim.
2 The headlamp contains a single bulb of the double filament type, to give an alternative dipped beam. The dip switch is on the left hand handlebar grip. A 15W/15W bulb is fitted to the S65 model. All other models use a 25W/25W bulb, taking advantage of the higher output from the generator. Some models have a separate pilot lamp.
3 It is not necessary to refocus the headlamp when a new bulb is fitted because the bulbs used are of the pre-focus type. To release the bulb holder from the reflector, pull from the locating flange.
4 Beam height is adjusted by means of the small screw immediately above the lamp rim retaining screw.

8 Stop and tail lamp - replacing bulbs

1 The rear lamp has a twin filament bulb of the 10W/3W type, to illuminate the rear of the machine and the rear number plate, and to give visual warning when the rear brake is applied. To gain access to the bulb, remove the two screws that retain the moulded plastics lens cover to the tail lamp assembly and remove the cover complete with sealing gasket.
2 If tail lamps keep blowing, suspect either vibration in the rear mudguard assembly, or a poor earth connection.
3 The stop lamp is operated by a stop lamp switch on the right hand side of the machine, immediately above the rear brake pedal. It is connected to the pedal by a spring, which acts as the operating medium. The body of the stop lamp switch is threaded, so that a limited range of adjustment is provided to determine when the lamp will operate.

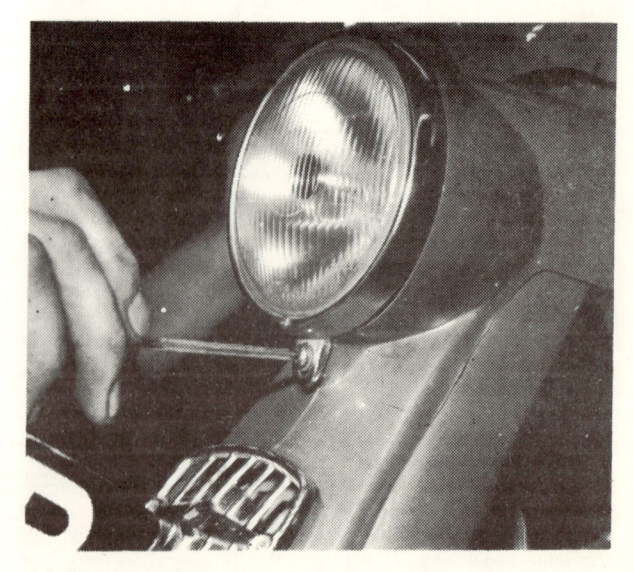

7.1. Bottom cross head screw releases headlamp front

7.3. Main bulb is retained by spring-loaded holder

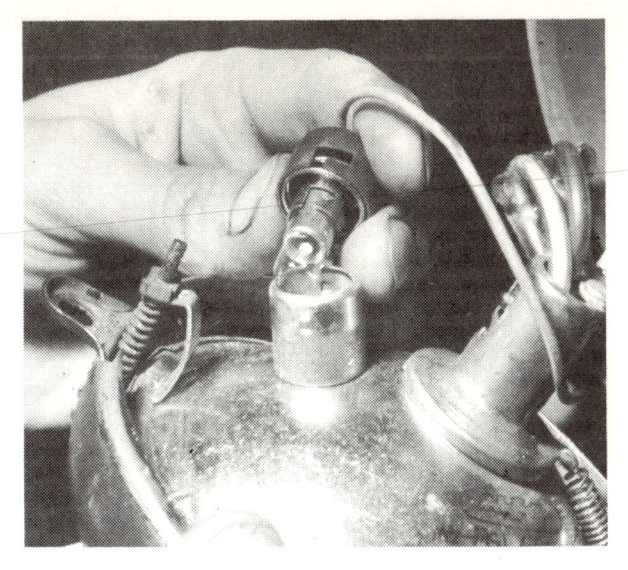

7.3A. Pilot bulb is a push fit in reflector

8.1. Slacken two cross head screws to remove lens cover

8.3. Body of stop lamp switch is threaded to aid adjustment

9 Flashing indicators - replacement of bulbs

1 The flashing indicators are located on the handlebar fairing of the scooter-type models and on the front forks of all other models. The rear-facing indicators are attached to the rear mudguard, below the seat or carrier.
2 In each case, access to the bulb is gained by removing the moulded plastics lens cover. Bulbs are rated at 8W; a special 'festoon' type is fitted to the handlebar fairing indicators that have an oblong lens cover.

10 Flasher unit - location and replacement

1 The flasher unit is located close to the battery, hanging vertically downwards from a single bolt fixing to the frame.
2 A series of audible clicks will be heard if the flasher unit is functioning correctly. If the unit malfunctions, the usual symptom is one initial flash before the unit goes dead. It will be necessary to replace the flasher unit complete if the fault cannot be attributed to either a burnt out indicator bulb or a blown fuse. Take care in handling the unit because it is easily damaged, if dropped.

11 Neutral indicator bulb - replacement

1 A neutral indicator light is incorporated in the headlamp shell, to show when the gear change lever is in neutral. A small contact in the gearbox selector drum provides the appropriate indication. Failure to indicate the selection of neutral can usually be attributed to a broken wire or a damaged contact.
2 The neutral indicator lamp is rated at 1.5W. It is a push fit into the rubber sleeve that holds it close to the green-coloured indicator glass.

12 Speedometer bulb - replacement

1 A 1.5W bulb is inserted from the bottom of the speedometer casing to illuminate the dial during the hours of darkness.

13 Horn - location and adjustment

1 The horn is located behind the metal grille above the front mudguard, which is attached to the plastics moulding carrying the headlamp shell that bridges the fork blades. The horn mounting bracket is bolted to two abutments projecting from

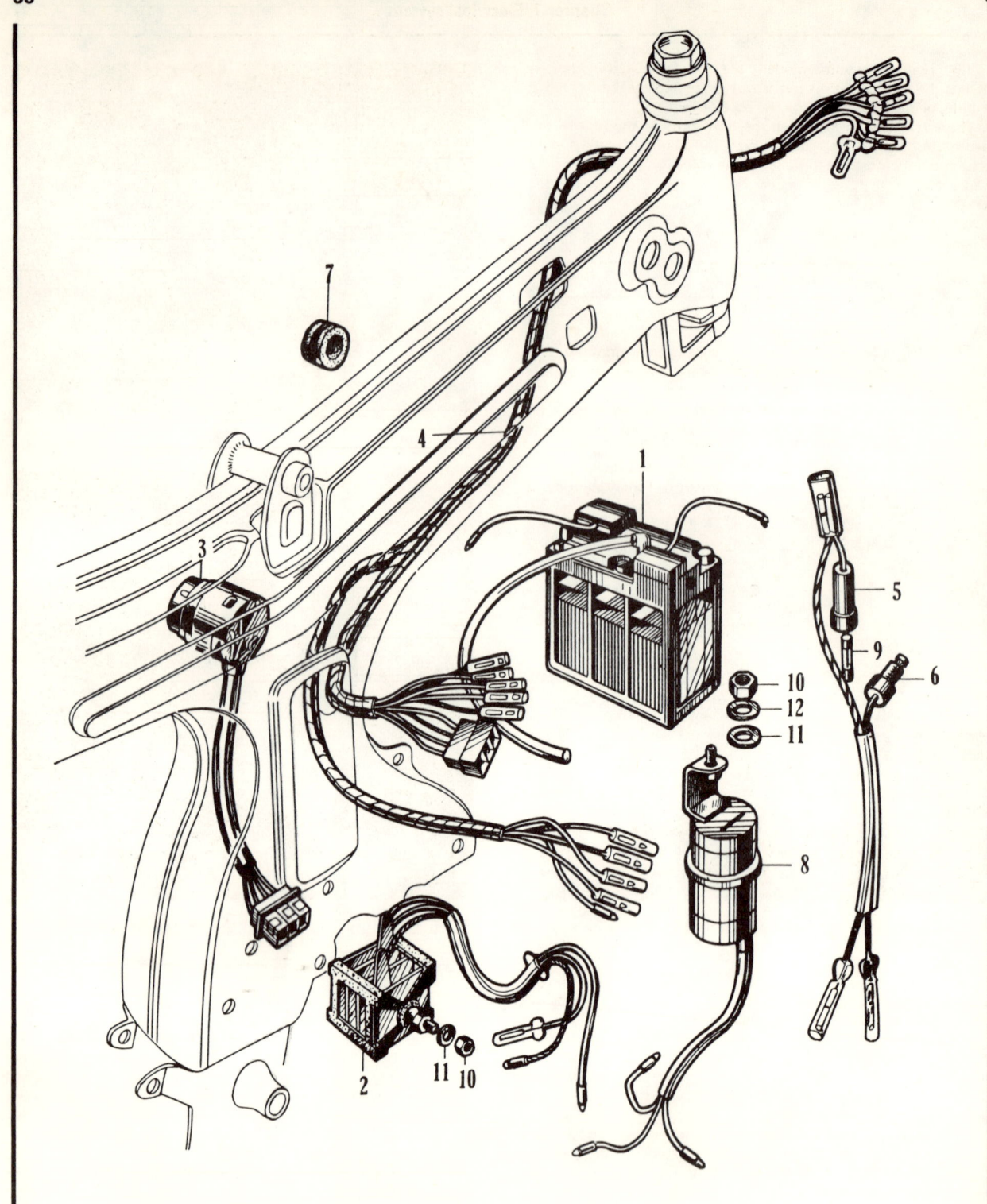

Fig. 7.1. Wiring harness and battery (Model S90 only)

1 Battery
2 Rectifier
3 Ignition/lighting switch
4 Wiring harness
5 Fuse holder
6 Detachable end of fuse holder
7 Grommet for wiring harness
8 Flasher unit
9 Fuse
10 Nut for flasher unit bracket and rectifier
11 Washer for flasher unit bracket and rectifier
12 Spring washer for flasher unit bracket

Note: Other models have a somewhat similar arrangement which may not correspond exactly with this diagram, due to differences in the circuit

Chapter 7/Electrical system

the fork blades. On some models, the horn is located in approximately the same position but is not protected by the moulding or grille, or is suspended from the air cleaner hose.

2 There is means of adjusting the horn note at the rear of the horn body. If the horn note is weak, the adjusting screw should be turned anticlockwise to increase the volume.

14 Ignition and lighting switch

1 The ignition and lighting switch is combined in one unit. It is operated by a key, which cannot be removed when the ignition is switched on.
2 The number stamped on the key will match the number on the lock. This will aid obtaining a replacement key, if the original is lost.
3 The ignition key operates also the steering head lock.
4 It is not practicable to repair the switch if it malfunctions. It should be replaced with another lock and key to match.

15 Wiring - layout and inspection

1 The wiring harness is colour-coded and will correspond with the accompanying wiring diagrams.
2 Visual inspection will show whether any breaks or frayed outer coverings are giving rise to short circuits. Another source of trouble may be the snap connectors, where the connector has not been pushed home fully in the outer housing.
3 Intermittent short circuits can often be traced to a chafed wire that passes through or close to a metal component, such as a frame member. Avoid tight bends in the wire or situations where the wire can become trapped between casings.

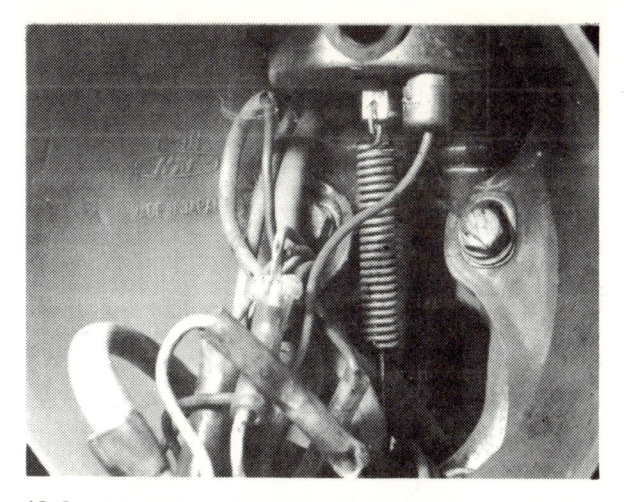

12. Speedometer bulb fits in bottom of casing

14.1. Ignition switch is behind left-hand cover

Schematic wiring diagrams begin overleaf

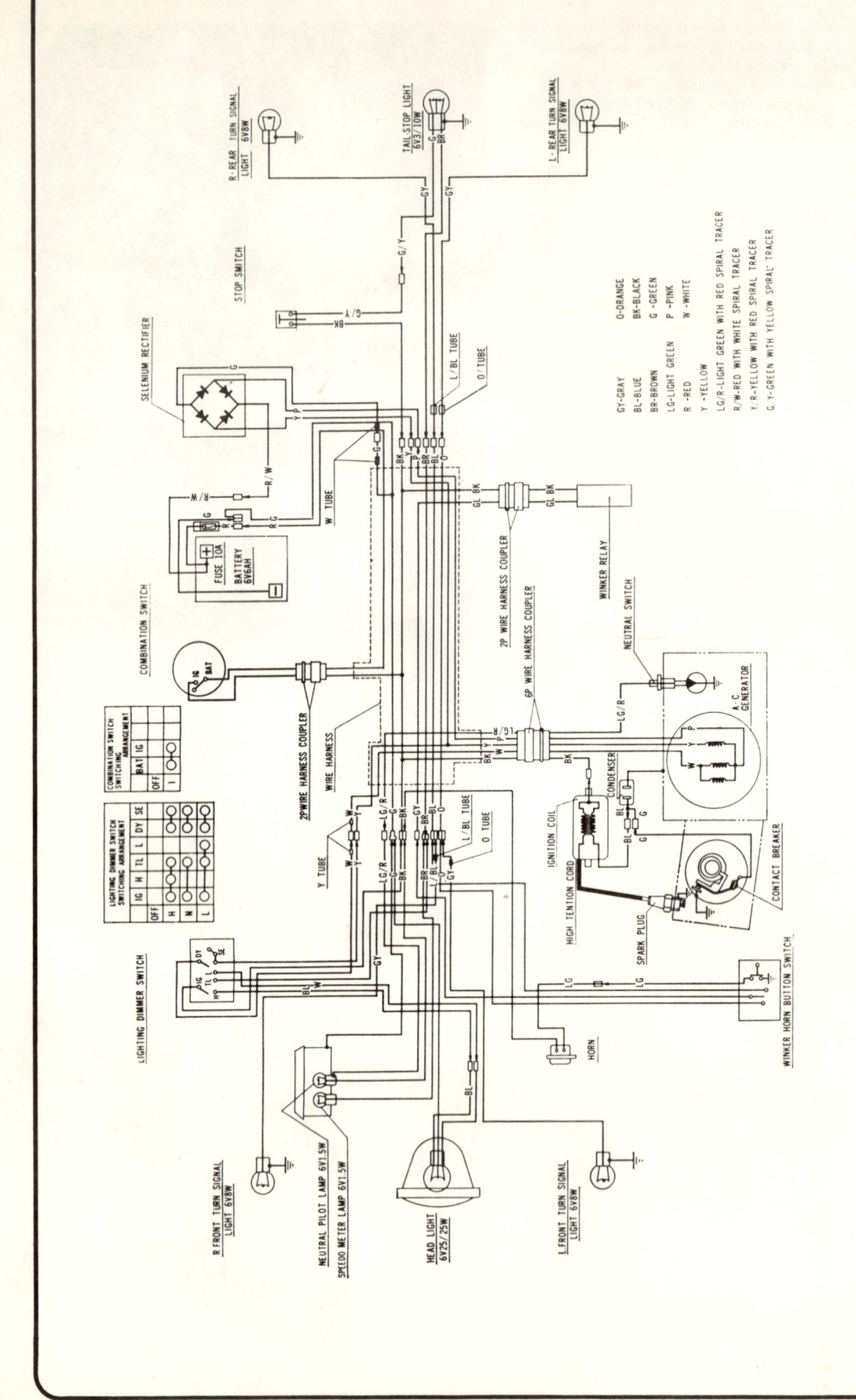

Honda S90 Schematic wiring diagram
(The S65 has a similar but not identical wiring layout)

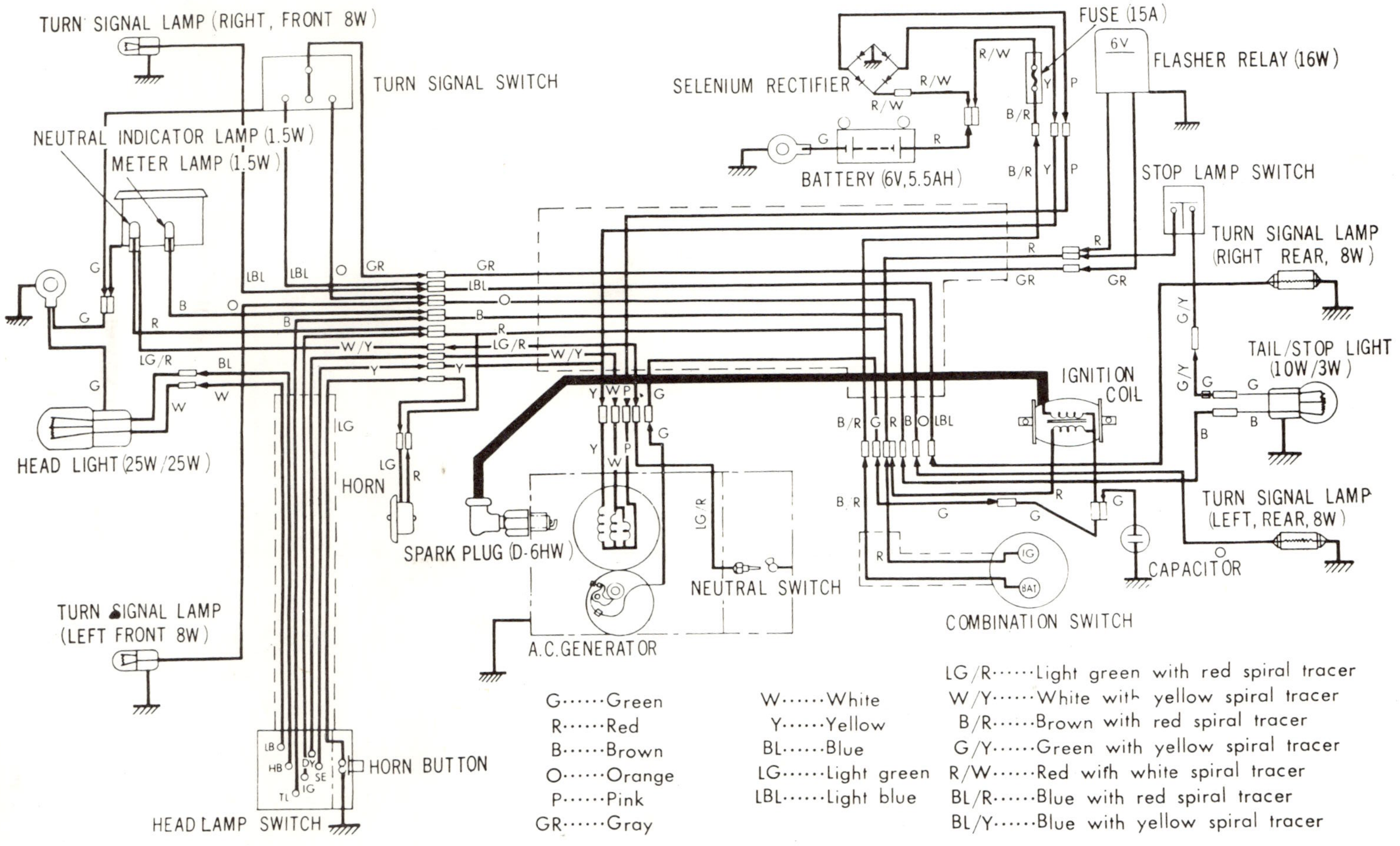

Honda C90 Schematic wiring diagram
(The C70 has a similar but not identical wiring layout)

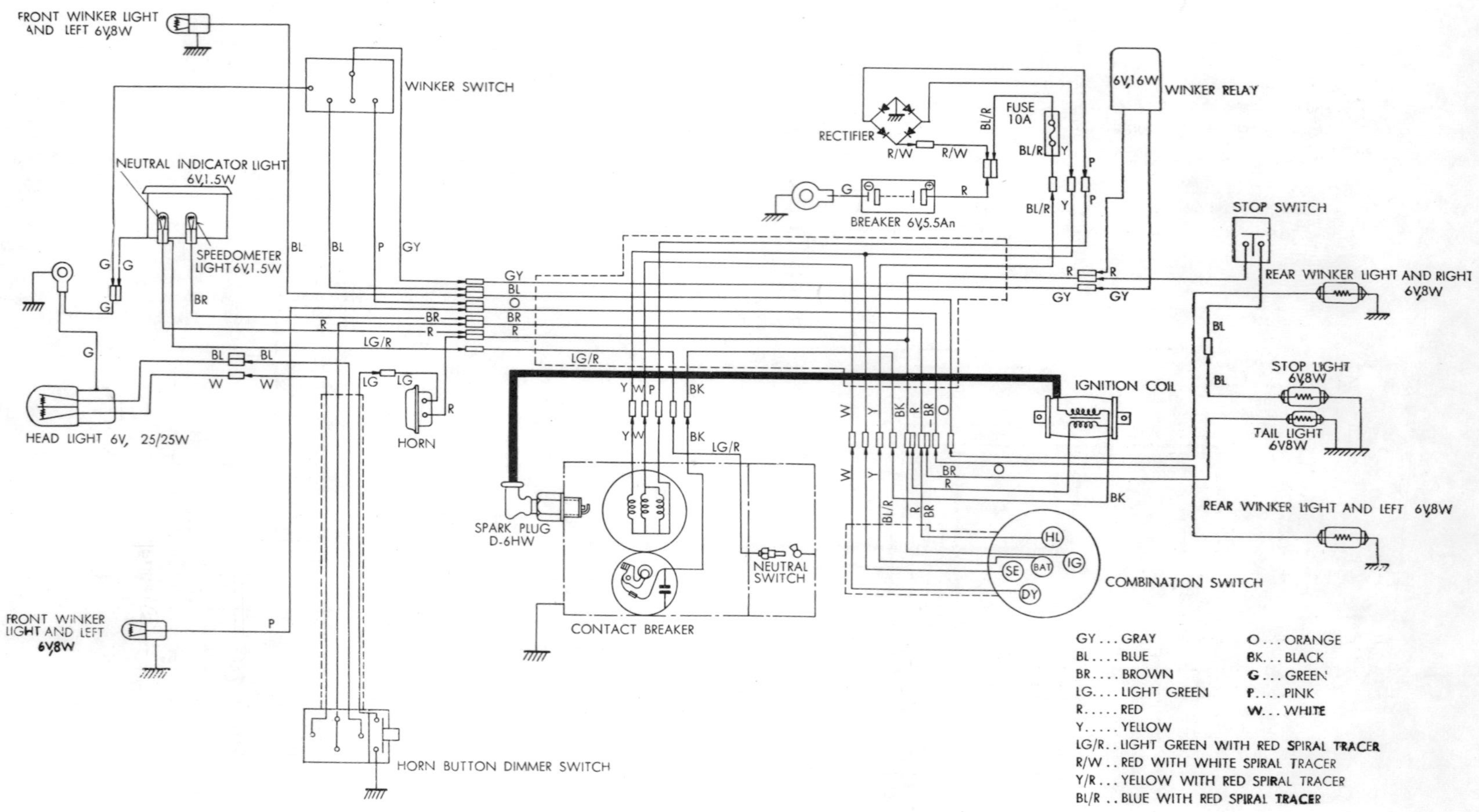

Honda CM90 Schematic wiring diagram

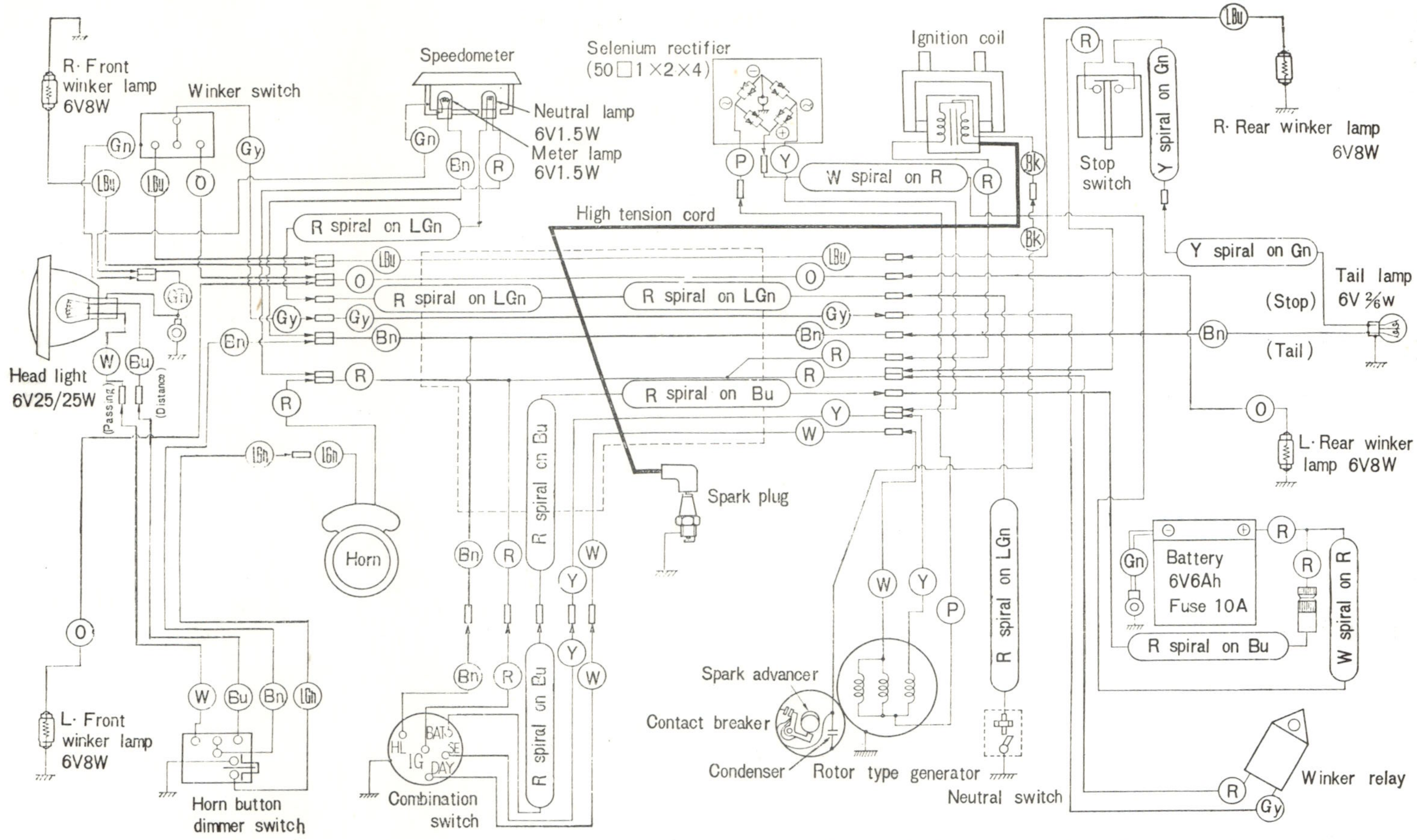

Honda C200   Schematic wiring diagram

Metric conversion tables

Inches	Decimals	Millimetres		Millimetres to Inches		Inches to Millimetres
			mm	Inches	Inches	mm
1/64	0.015625	0.3969	0.01	0.00039	0.001	0.0254
1/32	0.03125	0.7937	0.02	0.00079	0.002	0.0508
3/64	0.046875	1.1906	0.03	0.00118	0.003	0.0762
1/16	0.0625	1.5875	0.04	0.00157	0.004	0.1016
5/64	0.078125	1.9844	0.05	0.00197	0.005	0.1270
3/32	0.09375	2.3812	0.06	0.00236	0.006	0.1524
7/64	0.109375	2.7781	0.07	0.00276	0.007	0.1778
1/8	0.125	3.1750	0.08	0.00315	0.008	0.2032
9/64	0.140625	3.5719	0.09	0.00354	0.009	0.2286
5/32	0.15625	3.9687	0.1	0.00394	0.01	0.254
11/64	0.171875	4.3656	0.2	0.00787	0.02	0.508
3/16	0.1875	4.7625	0.3	0.01181	0.03	0.762
13/64	0.203125	5.1594	0.4	0.01575	0.04	1.016
7/32	0.21875	5.5562	0.5	0.01969	0.05	1.270
15/64	0.234375	5.9531	0.6	0.02362	0.06	1.524
1/4	0.25	6.3500	0.7	0.02756	0.07	1.778
17/64	0.265625	6.7469	0.8	0.03150	0.08	2.032
9/32	0.28125	7.1437	0.9	0.03543	0.09	2.286
19/64	0.296875	7.5406	1	0.03937	0.1	2.54
5/16	0.3125	7.9375	2	0.07874	0.2	5.08
21/64	0.328125	8.3344	3	0.11811	0.3	7.62
11/32	0.34375	8.7312	4	0.15748	0.4	10.16
23/64	0.359375	9.1281	5	0.19685	0.5	12.70
3/8	0.375	9.5250	6	0.23622	0.6	15.24
25/64	0.390625	9.9219	7	0.27559	0.7	17.78
13/32	0.40625	10.3187	8	0.31496	0.8	20.32
27/64	0.421875	10.7156	9	0.35433	0.9	22.86
7/16	0.4375	11.1125	10	0.39370	1	25.4
29/64	0.453125	11.5094	11	0.43307	2	50.8
15/32	0.46875	11.9062	12	0.47244	3	76.2
31/64	0.484375	12.3031	13	0.51181	4	101.6
1/2	0.5	12.7000	14	0.55118	5	127.0
33/64	0.515625	13.0969	15	0.59055	6	152.4
17/32	0.53125	13.4937	16	0.62992	7	177.8
35/64	0.546875	13.8906	17	0.66929	8	203.2
9/16	0.5625	14.2875	18	0.70866	9	228.6
37/64	0.578125	14.6844	19	0.74803	10	254.0
19/32	0.59375	15.0812	20	0.78740	11	279.4
39/64	0.609375	15.4781	21	0.82677	12	304.8
5/8	0.625	15.8750	22	0.86614	13	330.2
41/64	0.640625	16.2719	23	0.90551	14	355.6
21/32	0.65625	16.6687	24	0.94488	15	381.0
43/64	0.671875	17.0656	25	0.98425	16	406.4
11/16	0.6875	17.4625	26	1.02362	17	431.8
45/64	0.703125	17.8594	27	1.06299	18	457.2
23/32	0.71875	18.2562	28	1.10236	19	482.6
47/64	0.734375	18.6531	29	1.14173	20	508.0
3/4	0.75	19.0500	30	1.18110	21	533.4
49/64	0.765625	19.4469	31	1.22047	22	558.8
25/32	0.78125	19.8437	32	1.25984	23	584.2
51/64	0.796875	20.2406	33	1.29921	24	609.6
13/16	0.8125	20.6375	34	1.33858	25	635.0
53/64	0.828125	21.0344	35	1.37795	26	660.4
27/32	0.84375	21.4312	36	1.41732	27	685.8
55/64	0.859375	21.8281	37	1.4567	28	711.2
7/8	0.875	22.2250	38	1.4961	29	736.6
57/64	0.890625	22.6219	39	1.5354	30	762.0
29/32	0.90625	23.0187	40	1.5748	31	787.4
59/64	0.921875	23.4156	41	1.6142	32	812.8
15/16	0.9375	23.8125	42	1.6535	33	838.2
61/64	0.953125	24.2094	43	1.6929	34	863.6
31/32	0.96875	24.6062	44	1.7323	35	889.0
63/64	0.984375	25.0031	45	1.7717	36	914.4

Index

A

Adjusting tappets 29
Advance and retard mechanism 58
Air filter 54

B

Barrel 14, 20
Battery - maintenance 83
Battery - type 83
Big-end bearings 19
Brake adjustment 76
Brakes - specifications 71
Bulbs 84

C

Cam followers (ohv) 21
Camshaft (ohc) 34
Camshaft (ohv) 21
Camshaft chain tensioner (ohc) 38
Capacities 9
Carburettor 52
Centre stand 67
Chain - sizes 71
Cleaning 69
Clutch adjustment 50
Clutch - dismantling 47
Clutch operating mechanism 49
Clutch - specifications 47
Condenser 58
Connecting rod 17
Contact breaker - adjustment 57
Crankcase 17
Crankshaft 19
Cush drive assembly 76
Cylinder barrel 14, 20
Cylinder head 14, 34

D

Decarbonizing 20
Dry weight 5

E

Electrical system - specifications 83
Engine examination 19
Engine reassembly 21
Engine specifications 11, 31
Engine/gearbox removal 14, 32
Exhaust system 54
Exhaust valve 20, 36

F

Fault diagnosis - clutch 50
Fault diagnosis - engine 46
Fault diagnosis - frame and fork assembly 70
Fault diagnosis - fuel system 56
Fault diagnosis - gearbox 46
Fault diagnosis - ignition system 60
Fault diagnosis - wheels, brakes and final drive 82
Final drive 78
Flasher unit 85
Flashing indicators 85
Flywheel generator 57, 83
Footrests 67
Frame assembly 67
Frame number 6
Front brake - inspection 71
Front forks 61
Front wheel - inspection 71
Fuel system - specifications 51
Fuel tank 51
Fuses 84

G

Gear cluster 19
Gear selector drum 19
Generator 57, 83
Generator removal 14

H

Headlamp 84
Horn 85

I

Ignition coil 57
Ignition switch 87
Ignition system - specifications 57
Ignition timing 43
Indicators 85
Inlet valve 20, 36

K

Kickstarter ratchet 19
Kickstarter shaft 19

L

Layshaft assembly 19
Length 5
Lighting switch 84
Lubricants 9

M

Main bearings 19
Mainshaft assembly 19
Maintenance 7
Model range 5

N

Neutral indicator lamp 85

O

Oil change 7
Oil pump (ohc) 38
Oil seals 19
Overall length 5
Overall width 5

P

Petrol tank 51
Petrol tap 52
Piston 17, 20
Piston rings 17
Plastic moulding 59

R

Rear brake - inspection 75
Rear chain 78
Rear suspension units 67
Rear wheel 75
Rear wheel sprocket 76
Rings 17
Rockers 21
Rocker box 14
Rocker shafts 21, 46

S

Selenium rectifier 84
Seat 69
Sparking plug 58
Speedometer 67
Speedometer cable 67
Speedometer drive gearbox 69
Sprocket sizes 71
Steering head bearings 67
Steering head lock 67
Stop and tail lamp 84
Swinging arm 67

T

Timing 43
Timing pinions 21
Trochoid oil pump 38
Tyre removal and replacement 80
Tyre sizes 71

V

Valve grinding 20
Valve guides 20
Valves 17, 36
Valve seats 20
Valve timing (ohc) 43

W

Weight 5
Wheelbase 5
Wheel bearings 71
Wheels - specifications 71
Width 5
Wiring diagrams 88
Wiring harness 87

Printed by
J. H. HAYNES & Co. Ltd
Sparkford Yeovil Somerset